CLASSIC OUTDOOR
COLOR PORTRAITS
A Guide for Photographers

CLASSIC OUTDOOR
COLOR PORTRAITS

A Guide for Photographers

It's Your Turn to Make a Portrait

By

Nancy Hopkins Reily

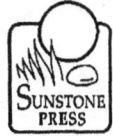

SUNSTONE
PRESS

Back cover:

Using Color for Portraiture
Part I: Color Wheel/Hues
Part II: Value Scale
Part III: Intensity Scale
Part IV: Selection of Portrait Color Scheme by Relationships
Part V: Selection of Clothes Color Scheme by Percentages

Sunstone books may be purchased for educational, business, or sales promotional use. For information please write: Special Markets Department, Sunstone Press, P.O. Box 2321, Santa Fe, New Mexico 87504-2321.

Library of Congress Cataloging-in-Publication Data:
Reily, Nancy Hopkins, 1934–
    Classic outdoor color portraits : a guide for photographers ; it's your turn to make a portrait / by Nancy Hopkins Reily.— 1st ed.
        p. cm.
    Includes index.
    ISBN: 0-86534-302-0
    1. Portrait photography—Handbooks, manuals, etc.   2. Outdoor photography—Handbooks, manuals, etc.   3. Portrait photography—Posing—Handbooks, manuals, etc. I. Title.

TR575 .R45 2001
778.9'2—dc21   00-030801

Published by SUNSTONE PRESS
                Post Office Box 2321
                Santa Fe, NM 87504-2321 / USA
                (505) 988-4418 / orders only (800) 243-5644
                FAX (505) 988-1025
                www.sunstonepress.com

DEDICATED TO:
My mother, Anna Pauline Richardson Hopkins Castleberry,
for her encouraging words,
"Nancy, always pursue your photography."

If photography beautifies reality,
I choose to begin with beauty.
The ordinary person, when
he reveals all his energy for the camera,
becomes an extraordinary person.

The reward is in the making of the portrait
and seeing the interest created.

CONTENTS

LIST OF ILLUSTRATIONS

PREFACE

The concept for this book began when Mary Johnston Read of Lufkin, Texas, encouraged me to conduct a workshop at Angelina College in Lufkin on the art of making classic color photographic portraits in outdoor settings. Now, I expand that workshop into another form—the written word.

The immediacy and convenience of a hand-held book for easy reference is the best forum for my thoughts. This "handbook" becomes my community "volunteer work" as I donate my experiences as an outdoor color portraitist. Also, I am freed from the repetition of teaching a class with specific hours and this allows me to pursue other creative endeavors.

Simply, I am organizing a few rules and guidelines that I have refreshed with my interpretations. In presenting a series of "building blocks" for a classic outdoor color portrait I express only my experiences. Every portraitist has different experiences resulting in various ways to photograph individuals in outdoor settings. The true subject is the beauty of the individual and everyone's approach varies. This handbook will serve every color portraitist and/or individual who photographs friends, clients, and family.

Photographic portrait work is paradoxical. The making of the portrait is easy because from the earliest man as he dwelled in caves to the present-day man, the individual has had the common desire to depict himself and as the individual changes, he follows his natural urge to record his own changing image, even if he considers himself "ordinary."

Being ordinary is being yourself with a distinct level of energy and inward power. When the individual releases that illusive, tiny part of his energized self, he is intimate for a fraction of a second with the camera to become extraordinary. That moment is when the complex components of the individual's energy, personality, physical presence, real or imagined history, and inner intensity collide and compress into a presentation of an individual fully in control of his life. As the subject's energy combines with the lighting and contacts the photographic film, a mystifying event happens to create an illusion that is not fully understandable, but accepted. As a portraitist you can bring forth this energized self if you possess the technical skills and passion.

I began my quest to make the ordinary individual extraordinary when I was seeking a creative outlet many years ago. An indescribable force within me wanted to say something that couldn't be said verbally. Early on I rejected the traditional creative outlets for women such as needlepoint and flower arranging. In 1970 when I finally showed an interest in photography, my husband Don gave me a fine camera. I was at an age when time had taught me the rhythms of life and the beat was fast. I bypassed all the mediocre seminars, popular magazines, and inferior equipment to concentrate on the best.

At first, I photographed individuals, then landscapes, insects, and still lifes and gave them to those who believed in me. Because I like people and respond to them one-on-one, I always returned to photographing individuals to find my highest reward. I photographed my family, then friends and finally photographed clients, many of whom I had not known previously. When I charged my clients a fee for the portrait some became my "critics" and they encouraged me to invest in myself by learning more skills.

Photography fit my needs in the early days because my children, Mark and Donna, were still at home. My time was somewhat fractured and photographing was squeezed in whenever possible. Then it took me years to develop my personal style, beginning with the first playful years of being fascinated and in love with photography, to studying the art of photography, and to developing precise techniques which challenged me and led to my style.

In September, 1979, the Museum of East Texas in Lufkin presented an exhibition, "Life The First Decade," with Doris C. O'Neil, Director of Vintage Prints for Time, Inc. While visiting with Doris I told her, "I know where my place is in the photography world." Doris replied, "Yes, others know more than you, but you know more than others."

I want to teach you what I know to stimulate you to tell me and others what you know. Now, take your camera out of the "never-ready" case. It's your turn to make classic outdoor color portraits.

And, although photography equipment and formats have changed from the earliest daguerreotypes to today's digital cameras, the basic concepts remain the same.

ACKNOWLEDGMENTS

I will always be indebted to Joseph Poulson Hedrick, Jr. and his wife, Mary Lou Thompson Hedrick, for giving of their time as Joe taught me the basics of portrait photography.

Teaching is an aggressive and generous effort. Respectful of the many who know more than me I thank those who taught and added to my accumulated knowledge: Ansel Adams, Gerhard Bakker, Ruth Bernhard, Don Blair, Lucien Clergue, Donald Jack, Leon Kennamer, Marvin Reese, Eugene Richards, Jack Sal, John Sexton, Michael Smith, Gail Skoff, Jim Twohig, Jerry Uelsmann, Ernest Wildi, Don Worth, and Joe Zeltsman.

My heartfelt gratitude to all who contributed their expertise in assembling this handbook: Georgiana Belaire, Amy Cook, Lucille Enix, Mary Frances Espinoza, Joyce Gray, Marilynn Green, Jonnie Sue Hill, Jeanelle McCall, J. P. McDonald, Mary Johnston Read, Julie Odom Rogers, Nancy Wilson, and the staffs of Angelina College Library and Kurth Memorial Library.

I extend my heartfelt thank you to the staff of Sunstone Press: Vicki Ahl and Brenda Meeks.

A congenial, competent publisher is the dream of all authors; in this respect I am quite fortunate to have James C. Smith, Jr. support my efforts with his ongoing perception, patience, and thoughtfulness.

A BEGINNING THOUGHT

You will be a better portraitist for reading about portraiture only to discover the true learning of the guidelines doesn't come before practice, but after.

CONCEPTS OF PORTRAITURE

Defining the Portrait

A portrait is a visual record of the whole or partial aspects of a person or persons as seen by another person. The portrait portrays a likeness from life in addition to rendering various moods such as glorifying, satirizing, and romanticizing. Regardless of the representation, if the person is identified or suggested, the image qualifies as a portrait.

The person making the classic outdoor color photographic portrait is you, the portraitist. The person being portrayed is the subject.

For this handbook I choose to portray the subject in a classic form suggesting accepted standards. For brevity, I refer to the classic outdoor color photographic portrait in a single term: the portrait.

To encourage you to develop skills that will enable you to become an extraordinary portraitist I have devised a series of "Building Blocks." Included in each building block are various concepts to bring forth from your "subconscious eye" a growing "conscious eye," to recognize and enjoy your response to things seen, and to encourage your limitless pursuit of portraiture.

"Building Blocks"

A working approach using the building blocks is to visualize the portrait format, whether a square, rectangle, circle, or oval as a flat surface with the imagined concept of layers of various building blocks placed so the two-dimensional surface builds to an illusionary three dimensions, Figure 1-1.

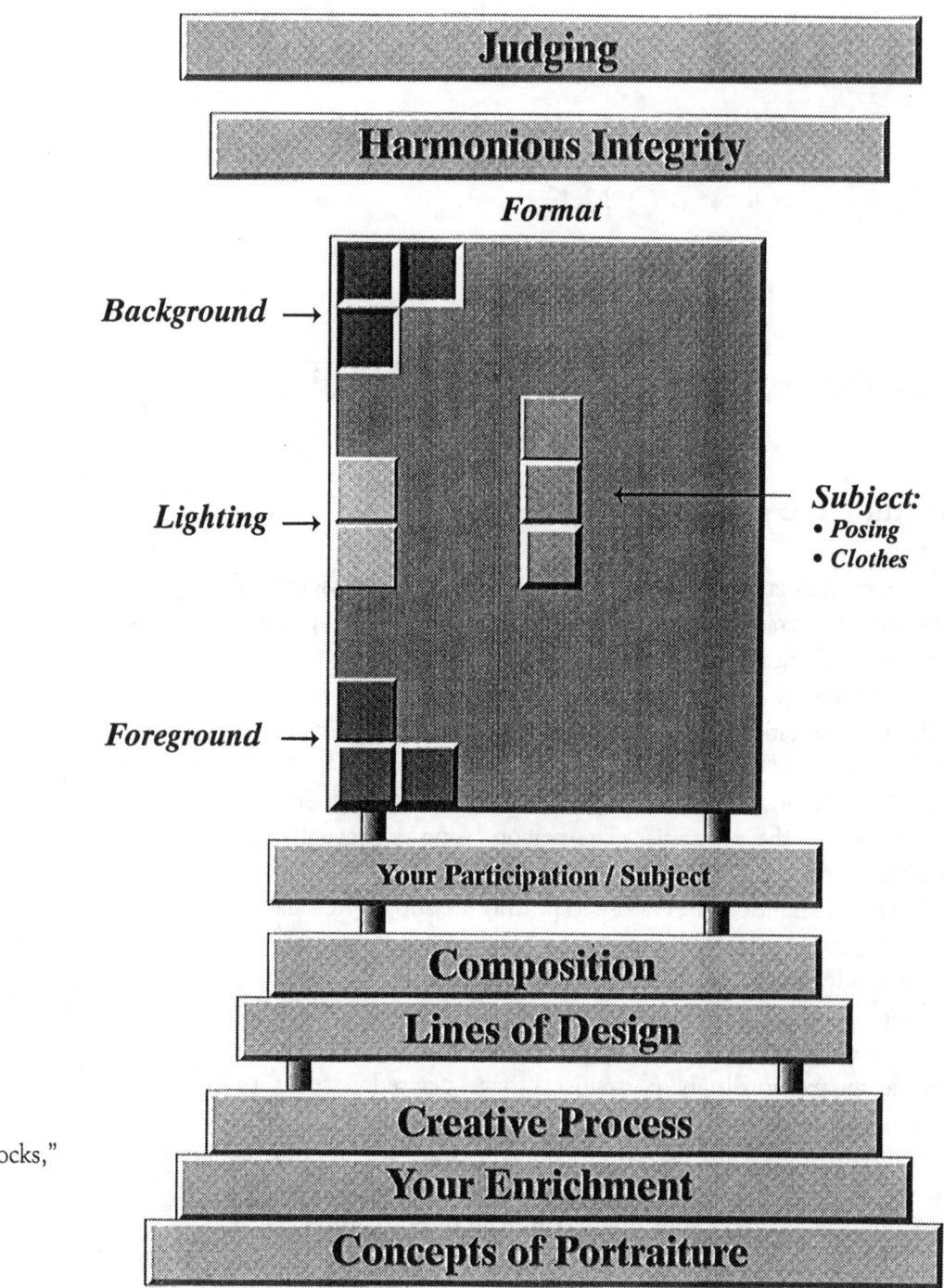

Figure 1-1
"Building Blocks,"
Front View

In Figure 1-1, visualize the front view of the format as a two-dimensional rectangle of length and width supported by foundation building blocks of the Concepts of Portraiture, Your Enrichment, and Creative Process.

The Concepts of Portraiture is communication in a particular time and space enriched by the era, nation, or culture. In doing so the portrait conveys actual and emotional dimensions in transcribing a three-dimensional subject into a two-dimensional form. All portraiture is worth studying because the past communicates what and how portraits have been made; the present helps us discover what and how portraits are made today.

The portrait is enhanced by understanding of Your Enrichment building blocks of seeing, intellect, perception, intuition, observation, imagination, anticipation, and expression. The result is a more refined portrait as if viewing the portrait not only from the front flat surface but from all perspectives. I present exercises later in the handbook to develop the application of these enriching building blocks.

The Creative Process clarifies how imaginative thoughts and skills evolve into a portrait. Again, exercises are presented later in the handbook.

The next two foundation building blocks of Lines of Design and Composition further support the portrait by your envisioning the portrait construction.

With the support foundation properly laid the actual work on the portrait begins with Your Participation when you engineer the lighting, foreground, and background. At the same time the middle ground is considered when the subject participates with you by posing and selecting clothes.

As all efforts are assembled the building blocks are placed under a canopy of Harmonious Integrity which is your style of portraiture. Lastly, every building block is critiqued by Judging.

As all these building blocks are formed and bound together the format evolves from two dimensions to an illusionary three dimensions as shown in Figure 1-2.

A classic portrait is not made by accident but by the careful study and visualization of all the involved building blocks. The poverty of visualizing is not characteristic of fine portraiture. In this search for fine relationships among all the building blocks opportunities for choices exist. The better the choices, the better the portrait.

The presentation of these building blocks is like a workshop in your home and, hopefully, the study is an ongoing experience rather than a one-time event. I endeavor to supply you with enough information in addition to exciting inspiration so the mastering of this handbook is not the end of your making portraits but the beginning with your advancing the information and inspiration to a higher level of expressive communication.

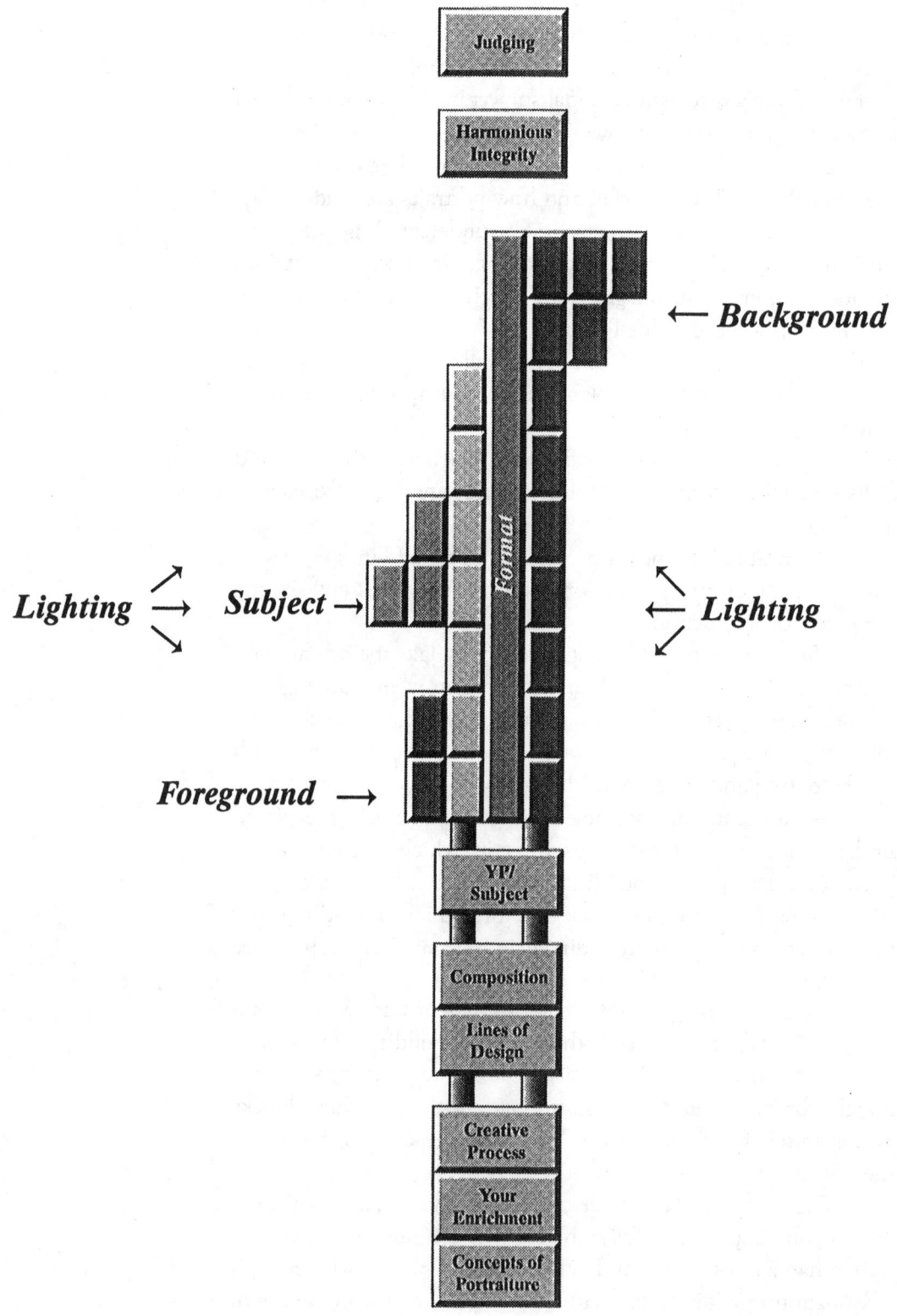

Figure 1-2
"Building Blocks," Side View

The Portrait as a Form of Communication

The basic concept of portraiture consists of the age-old concept of communication. The transmitting of information is how communication meets a person's need to express an idea and emotion to another person.

Speech, by spoken words and gesture of body movements, formed mankind's first attempt to communicate. Speech with its companion, gesture, lasts only for a moment and is lost after performed. In duration the camera's moment of a "seeing" eye resembles speech and gesture but is retrievable.

Early man in his insatiable desire for better communication drew miniature objects on cave walls. These "portraits" merely acknowledged an object's existence with no effort to interpret the portrayed elements. They were similar to the elementary portrait, the static daguerreotype which offered no explanations, only acknowledged the subject. Later the cave dweller added an illusion of depth to the drawings by using the protrusions and recessions in the walls.

Man furthered communication with writing skills of hieroglyphics on clay tablets. As the phonetic system of writing emerged man's attempt to communicate took on human qualities of motion and emotion.

As the technical skills of the early photographer developed so did his skill of showing perspective, emotion, motion, and intent. This redefined reality of the camera's eye changed as the portraitist envisoned what could be enhanced by subduing or emphasizing.

Regardless of the era, nation, or culture portraiture reflects the quality, character, and achievements of the subject and serves as another way to write biographies.

Dimensions In Portraiture

Art is either two dimensional or three dimensional with the difference being the concept of space. Three-dimensional art, such as architecture and sculpture, exists as an "in the round" form occupying actual length, width, and depth. In three-dimensional art, the subject is viewed from all angles. Two-dimensional art, such as painting or photographic portraiture, exists on a flat surface occupying length and width with depth as an illusion created by the artist. Two-dimensional art requires viewing the flat surface from a single viewpoint. The actual subject is altered when the subject's image is placed on a two-dimensional surface to become a static, flat surface instead of an "in the round" body.

In addition to physical dimensions a portrait emphasizes a subject's emotional appearance which is the visual excitement created by his inward energy and your ability to show length, width, and depth.

Emotional Dimensions

The subject, you, and the viewer are involved in creating visual excitement. The subject chooses to reveal his unseen information. You instinctively listen to your emotions and determine what you want before the "moment of truth" disappears. You photograph the expression you feel but don't see. The viewer, an essential element of a portrait, usually views the portrait without guidance, because a portrait avoids titles except for the person's name. You are a good portraitist when your skills appear so easy that the viewer assumes the viewer can make the same portrait.

Three-Dimensional Forms

The three-dimensional forms in art work are actually defined as the four dimensions of actual space with all encompassing points as shown in Figure 1-3. To speak of these four dimensions for artistic purposes, means these four dimensions are a "three-dimensional concept."

These points exist in time with the addition of movement which is dealt with artistically by illusion.

Time, a "fifth" dimension, is added to further elaborate on the other dimensions because the time of day with its various colorations—yellow at sunrise, red at sunset—adds dimension to space. The concept of time, relating to dimension, moves at a steady day-to-day pace bringing sun-giving lighting.

When representing a three-dimensional object on a flat surface I direct you to recognize what you are attempting to accomplish by exploring the representation of the human form as constructed by a sculptor.

The sculptor creates a portrait by working in space with tangible materials of weight and mass to create volume. The chosen materials have their characteristics such as clay which is additive or marble which is subtractive. The weight of the solid form is felt and established by flat or rounded planes that push into space as if writing. The sculpting of the human form relates to the front, back, and sides continuously. The sculptor shows movement because the human form even in repose expresses movement with breath and pulse beat. The environment is included in a sculptor's execution

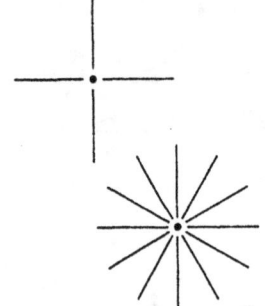

Figure 1-3
All Dimensions

because the human lives with interior and exterior landscape, atmosphere, and lighting. All the avenues of sculpture deal with the various intentions, personality, and sensitivities of the sculptor.

If the sculpture stands free of support on all sides the sculpture is "in the round" and is considered the most exact replica of the three-dimensional form.

If the sculpture is minimally supported with almost all the surrounding edges removed, the sculpture is called "free standing."

If the sculpture is supported maximally as in an embossed surface, the sculpture is called a "relief sculpture." Relief sculpture carved in a flat surface manner is called "low relief." Relief sculpture carved in a very rotund and high manner is called "high relief."

When in the round, free standing, and relief sculpture from high relief to low relief are placed side by side, the convergence of three dimensions to two dimensions is easily seen with shadows, lighting, and perception. In addition, contrast, repetition, and continuity duplicate life's forms and entice the viewer's eye.

Two-Dimensional Forms

The portraitist works in two dimensions and doesn't duplicate life's forms. Mass exists only in nature and in three-dimensional art.

Life is easier to comprehend by placing life on a flat, two-dimensional surface because life on a flat surface appears more manageable, compact, and less threatening. When the inner space of the self-contained person resides on a flat surface the viewer is not overwhelmed.

Three-dimensional sculptures of human forms are touched and observed from all angles, but when the human form is photographed all of the human form is not available to view. In Western art, photographic portraiture is perceived as the most realistic depiction of a person. Yet, there is a side that you can't see and must assume, in the mind's eye, to see—the other side of the person. A portraitist represents only a part of the total. The way you represent the part that isn't seen becomes your concern only.

The Perspective of History

To understand where portraiture is today and its direction tomorrow, an examination of the past as represented by history is helpful. History provides a passage of time from the portrait of any era, nation, or culture and permits the viewer to make a fresh interpretation about what is noteworthy. Time clears the viewer's eye by distancing the viewer's emotions. Then portraiture is placed in context with culture's influential events, spirit, and the development of ideas regarding religion, nudity, intellect, magic, superstition, the treatment of men, women, and children, the emergence of the ruling class and common people and, finally, who influenced the portraitist. All this gives clues to the value of aesthetics, discipline, self-restraint, and standards that reveal ambitions, humility, and sympathetic handling of human frailties.

To study past portraiture allows you to see the development regarding posing, perception, theme, subject matter, lighting, shadow, movement, clothes, expression, foreground, background, portrait size, and lines of design. Also included are techniques, patrons, markets, available materials, and depositories such as tombs, museums, homes, corporation offices, and palaces. But the most important aspect of studying past portraiture is to see the images as beautiful.

These past portraits aren't lifeless works of art, but "alive" art of their time relating how individuals lived and what ruled their spirit. From these developments trends are formed and over a period of time the trends form a rhythm. When the rhythm swings to an extreme, the rhythm eventually swings in an opposite direction forming another rhythm and trend.

Many ideas have a natural beginning at the start of an artistic movement and continue to the movement's climax and demise. However, in studying art history, the history of every era begins with an outburst of art in an instantaneous explosion of energy. When the art explosion receives acceptance, the explosion diminishes. This process repeats and repeats throughout history. The classic rhythms are strengthened with each new interpretation.

When photography began in the mid 1800s, the first photographic portraiture adhered closely to the painter's tradition. Naturally, the study was of available portraiture which included drawings, oil portraiture, and sculpture.

I make no attempt in this handbook to present the history of portraiture. I only want to recommend the value of studying portraiture because the finer points are gathered from all sources.

For example, the drawings on the cave dweller's walls were a miniaturization of the single figure and showed how he manipulated his world. He believed that to paint man's portrait was to steal his image or soul and that the portrait drawn on the wall harmed the person. These early beliefs prevented portraiture from becoming a prevailing art form. Today some Native Americans or people of certain religious beliefs won't allow their photograph made because they believe the camera steals their image.

In Egypt, circa 3100 BC, the cave wall had been abandoned. Attempts were being made to show movement by sculpting one foot forward and seating the individual with criss-crossed legs to introduce a diagonal line of design.

Greece introduced the beginning of personalities in their portraiture and presented man as perfection. In Greek sculpture, each part of the body participated and compensated for every other part of the body in the pull with gravity. Counterposing was accomplished by weight shifting of the foot, knee, leg, and hip.

The climax of all portraiture that relates to today's portraiture originated during the period from 1300 to 1600 known as the Renaissance. This period which followed the Middle Ages marked the rebirth of classical antiquity.

The Impressionists in the late nineteenth century broke away from tradition and introduced emotional expressions. Into this climate the photograph was introduced. The oil portraitist, as a result of photography, painted reflected light. Photography offered a release for the oil portraitist because he no longer was solely responsible for recording the world's individuals, thus allowing the artist freedom to paint in an expressive manner. In time oil portraiture and photography became intertwined as the oil portraitist turned to photography for preliminary sketches.

I am not setting forth a history of the photographic portrait. With the following few examples I am suggesting your study of past photographic portraitists: Albert J. Southworth (1811-1894), a daguerreotypist whose portraits were spontaneous; Josiah J. Hawes (1808-1908), whose portraits revealed sensitivities not revealed in the prevailing portraits by using lighting, posing, and backgrounds artificially; Julia Margaret Cameron (1815-1879), who purposefully photographed public personalities out-of-focus and said, "Who has the right to say what focus is a legitimate focus"?; Joseph Karsh (1908-2002), whose classical lighting of persons who made a difference in the world fulfilled the public's insatiable desire to know of the famous.

Studying past portraiture offers both the amateur and professional portraitist inspiration because the nature of portraiture, whether active or passive, represents a piece of life. An intense study of portraiture reveals insights that people saw and felt about other people. These insights provide a collective way of seeing others and confirm that portraiture mirrors the self.

For you, history acts as a reference point that links today's cultural traditions with the portraits of the "great masters." The point of studying the historical development of portraiture isn't to imitate or copy an oil portrait or sculpture, but to learn how the great masters used the elements. However, you must recognize that these great masters' works reflected a different time and space. Today you compare work with your peers, but a worthwhile comparison is with the great masters whose judgments have passed the test of time. Since today's portrait becomes history tomorrow, past portraits should be viewed with today's sensitivities.

The Present Form of the Portrait

Today, the photographic biography of a person is represented by a snapshot, candid portrait, and formal portrait.

The snapshot is accessible, inexpensive, and popular. It has a proper and legitimate place as a record made by a person of scant visual ambition with a minimum level of expertise.

The untutored snapshot depicts social situations that give historical descriptions with emphasis on the subject rather than making a visual statement. Without an explanation, the viewer interprets the snapshot as he chooses.

The snapshot is usually a souvenir of an ordinary but particular time and space. The amateur's passion for life demands a record of what he experiences. The "ordinary" person photographed in a snapshot as he paused to celebrate a birthday or vacation, or the person caught in an unguarded moment can result in something extraordinary.

A family owned camera allows for photographing the family on holiday as an activity of the family's time together. Usually one person is missing in a group of two or more because of his role as "portraitist."

Most snapshots are not for public display but for private collections.

A snapshot records "today" so that "tomorrow" one can demonstrate what yesterday looked like. It provides a certainty so each generation can know how they looked at each stage of life. People know what their grandparents and even great-grandparents looked like in the "single study" snapshot.

The candid portrait had its beginning in the snapshot, is more than just a visual record, and is a portrait stripped to the essentials. It shows life in a pure form—an unguarded moment—made objectively by accident. The technique is secondary to spontaneity and intuition.

The small, modern-day, hand-held cameras give snapshots and candid portraiture their popularity. Portraiture becomes a reflexive activity rather than the time-consuming process in the beginning days of photography when only the inventors took photographs with no apparent social use. There were no professionals, hence no amateurs. Today both professionals and amateurs enjoy popularity.

The formal portrait commands a proper place in the visual diary because of the portraitist's active observation and participation in the subject's vulnerability. The formal portrait is made "by permission" while the candid is made or "stolen" without permission. This formal portrait can change our view of a person whereas a snapshot and candid might not do so.

A formal portrait on a single frame of film shows an exact moment of a person's life, a "still life." This exact moment has motion before and after. The motion in this still life continues when additional single frames of the same subject displaying different poses, lighting, and perception are taken at the same time and are placed in a row.

The formal portrait records a person in his "time" and reflects his culture. The formalness explains a person to his fellow persons with human emotions taking on a visible form that can be observed by large numbers of people today and tomorrow.

The formal portrait is made primarily for the family, but appeals beyond the family. Formal portraits convey meaning that non-family members can appreciate and bring pleasure to the viewer who may not know the person.

The album of snapshots, candids, and formal portraits, as a work of art itself, assures longevity. The album has a wider circulation than a portrait hanging on the wall because a portrait on the wall means people must come to a particular location and this limits those who can view the portrait.

The album full of snapshots, candids, and formal portraits is a portable gallery or museum with no walls or visiting hours. The album becomes part of a storage system that not everyone will see. Yet, the album is a means of recording that rivals the written word as a storage system.

These portraits placed in an album allow the average man to present himself to society in a time-study as he sees himself. Extended over time the album demonstrates infancy, youth, middle age, and old age with moods such as humor, sadness, eloquence, casualness, wonderment, and naivety. The statement declares the subject was here, an achievement not available in other art forms.

Because families are often separated in time and space, portraits placed in a family album show a family's connectedness.

The album often records the only time family members are together.

The snapshots and candids in an album can be in sequence of action, but there is no assurance they will be viewed in that order. As the album is viewed repeatedly, the viewer feels like he knows the people and their stories. With the passage of time the album is often lost and arrives at anonymity in antique and collectible stores, even flea markets. At this point the album becomes a chronicler of the times of ordinary people and earns extraordinary respect by biographers.

·-T W O -·

YOUR ENRICHMENT

Defining Enrichment

To enrich is to make finer by supplying additional elements. Knowing how to operate your camera and equipment is essential but using your camera artistically is accomplished with enrichment.

For your personal enrichment I suggest exploring these "building blocks": seeing, intellect, perception, intuition, observation, imagination, anticipation, and expression. These elements singly require study to assemble them as a whole. After each building block I have provided exercises for further study.

Seeing

To "see" is to acquire knowledge and understanding through the eye. Of the five senses—seeing, hearing, tasting, touching, and smelling—the most knowledge is absorbed through the eye.

Sight is a function, but seeing is an art requiring more than looking which is a less complicated, casual glance. To see is to understand and be a participant in that which is seen.

The many elements involved in seeing at a level of comprehension essential for a portraitist begins early in life. An infant perceives with curiosity only light with various colors and intensities. As an infant's sight develops, the ability to focus on objects develops and advances to the fixed seeing of an adult.

Over time intuition becomes part of the natural seeing process. Then, by adding intellect, perception, observation, imagination, anticipation, and expression, the mature person developing into a portraitist, observes with intuition and a trained, seasoned eye. The human eye is now more than just a means to look at objects.

Actually, seeing is a means of communication using images which can't be fixed the same way the camera fixes images. Seeing is an expression of visual thought that results in visual images. This is similar to how speech communicates as an expression of verbal thought that results in spoken images. These visual images add to your reasoning ability and act as the connecting elements that allow your mind to leap back and forth, a subconscious process that feeds your mind with what is known.

The beginner portraitist thinks naively that there is only one way to see, but the mature portraitist knows he sees what he learns to see.

Because each person is unique as to what he sees, each is trained to see and collect information differently.

Seeing is a talent that you gladly accept. If seeing arrives only by intellect, your passion is missing. If seeing is with your heart, your passion illuminates the portrait and the viewer will recognize the passion.

Exercise 1

To practice structured seeing, look at the cartoon panel, "Hocus Focus," in your newspaper comic section. "Hocus Focus" offers two drawings and instructs you to find a certain number of differences between the panels. To check your accuracy, the drawing reveals the answers.

Exercise 2

Become a "people watcher" to fine tune the art of seeing. In any place where people gather, select a person to watch. Try not to be too obvious. Make notes in a notebook describing attire, facial and body characteristics, mannerisms, attitude, and behavior. Jot down how you would photograph the person as to camera angle, lighting, foreground, background, and posing.

As your notebook fills, you will find the descriptions become easier. Gradually you develop a new insight into people and discover that each person requires a different technique to photograph.

Exercise 3

Make a roll of black and white negative film with prints to study the light.

Exercise 4

For the beginning portraitist, lighting may be the last factor in his experience. But the experienced portraitist knows that lighting is the most important element in a portrait because the basis of photography is light. Harsh, direct sun creates different lighting patterns than soft, open shade lighting.

Study the lighting on the face and body by asking a patient friend to stand in the following positions:

- Inside an outside doorway in the direct sun facing you as you stand outside the doorway
- Inside an inside doorway in the open shade facing you as you stand outside the doorway

Now ask the friend to assume these various positions:

- By a dark colored door
- By a light colored door
- With the door half open
- With the door fully open
- With the body at a 45 degree angle
- With the body at a full frontal angle
- With the face at a 45 degree angle
- With the face at a full frontal angle, use a black reflector on the side of face away from the door; use a white reflector on the side of face away from the door; use a black reflector above the head; use a white reflector in front of the subject.

Exercise 5

A useful way to "see" is to focus your vision onto a smaller, more manageable area by using an empty cardboard slide mount format as in Figure 2-1.

If you work with a 35mm camera, use that size empty slide mount format. If you use a 2 1/4 x 2 1/4 format, use that size empty slide mount format.

Paint the empty cardboard slide mount format black on all sides and edges. Use black because black reflects light poorly. Differences in blacks vary: matte black gives a gray cast; glossy black gives a darker black; and lacquered or wet black gives the blackest black.

Hold the black, empty cardboard slide mount format to one eye, with the other eye closed. This is the way your camera sees. If you want, keep both eyes open, because this is the way your eyes see. But, the best way is to close one eye.

Hold the slide mount format at any distance from your eye to simulate the desired lens size. If held approximately eight inches from the eye, the slide mount format simulates a normal lens. If held further than eight inches from the eye, a telephoto lens is simulated. If held closer than eight inches to the eye, a wide angle lens is simulated.

Record the distances you hold the slide mount format from the eye and the exact boundaries of the format. Then count and record the objects in your format. Now observe and list each category such as colors, forms, and lighting. Also, group objects by texture, function, and light and dark. Later, repeat the exercises at

Figure 2-1
Empty Cardboard Slide Mount
Format

the same location and distance from the eye to see what you missed. Add these to your list. This allows you to see objects in a different way instead of the usual, familiar viewpoint such as a tree is a tree and a fence is a fence.

As you observe everything in your slide mount format, vary what you see by moving the format to include planes of foreground, middle ground, and background. Next tilt the bottom of the slide mount format forward, then tilt the bottom of the slide mount format backward. Position the slide mount format at low and high camera angles. Move closer to isolate and fragment the subject. Use the slide mount format during different times of the day to study the various lighting.

As a result of these exercises, everything in your mind is in a frame with the slide mount format. If you learn to "see" with this format you soon won't need a frame or want one because you seldom view the world in a framed manner.

Intellect

The intellect begins where the senses stop. Intellect involves the power of the mind to understand, think, and acquire knowledge as distinguished from what is felt. Mathematics is the purest form of intellect.

To be intellectual is to understand ideas and rationally solve problems. This is called reasoning which guides behavior.

Thinking is objective, or influenced by positive or negative elements such as hope, creativity, control, organization, uselessness, destructiveness, lack of restraint, and disorganization.

IQ tests measure the rational part of the mind which includes math and verbal skills. From person to person intelligence is rated high, average, or low. To score high on an IQ test doesn't automatically insure success in every aspect of life. (Far from it.) IQ tests measure what is a good basis for being successful in life, but don't measure the practical elements of intelligence such as persuasion, managing yourself, ability to seek information, problem solving, strategic planning, and making the best of one's talents. These aspects of intelligence are learned by enhancing different aspects of practical intelligence.

Intellect isn't to be confused with wisdom. Wisdom is the use of knowledge and experience. Wisdom involves a sense of perspective as a result of gathering information from all past and present viewpoints. If communicated to others, this information is available for reflection. Wisdom is spiritual rather than quick-witted intelligence. Wisdom allows the understanding of other avenues of life which results in placing events in proper perspective.

Intellect includes the ability to assemble many areas of knowledge and develop a new approach. This is known as creative thinking.

Personality defines how a person uses their intellect. Some personalities prefer to think within set boundaries, some initiate projects that have new boundaries, and some prefer to critique and evaluate. Intelligence explains why persons perform with different levels of success when confronted with the same problem.

Heredity and environment contribute and control intelligence. Heredity is what is passed from parents to a person and is not negotiable. The environment is determined by, among other elements, the amount of formal or informal education a person receives.

With intelligence, you can place the sum of your motivation, direction, temperament, and character into a portrait.

Your emotions, instincts, and feelings provide energy or drive for behavior. This constitutes motivation.

Your intellect, with perceptual ability, guides behavior toward conscious or subconscious goals. This constitutes direction.

You receive temperament, the mixture of all your characteristics, from heredity.

You acquire character, the composite of moral qualities, after birth.

To establish the right balance of intellect and intuition, each exists with the elements of observation, perception, imagination, anticipation, and expression. These elements blend in the art of creativity.

Exercise 6

Read books on photography and other books that appeal to you. Study to advance your knowledge. Attend concerts and lectures. Do anything that stimulates your mind.

Perception

Perception, as a part of intelligence, is the system of processing awareness and the understanding of something through the senses and their sensations.

The senses function without learning, but perception improves with training. From birth, perception develops rapidly for the next seven or eight years and then levels out to remain constant until advancing age.

For your purposes as a portraitist, seeing is the sense of primary concern. Information is received and placed into perception. Your response to perception is determined by how complex the information is; the more complex the information, the more complex the response. Even more time is required if judging is added to response time.

Several avenues of response that classify the information into memory are open to you. If what is seen is new to you and not stored in your mind's classifying system, your mind takes a long time to perceive the object or event. Your mind then sorts the information. To accept the new information, perception expands slowly by adding new categories. But, if you see the same object over and over your perception responds quickly and you don't pay much attention to the process.

If you prepare your mind to see something, your mind preconceives the event into your classifying system and then perception requires minimum effort.

With adequate perception you can visualize your portrait clearly in your mind before making the portrait. This visualization is your freedom to express.

Exercise 7

A simple exercise to confirm differences in perception is for several portraitists to look at a subject and the surroundings. When each portraitist relates his version of what he sees, no two portraitists perceive alike.

Intuition

Intuition is the ability to know something without thinking it through and not knowing why. A subject or event doesn't require study to know something because intuition allows an immediate, spontaneous understanding. Intuition can't be taught and is the opposite of intellect. The purest form of intuition is "feeling."

Creative persons have a tension between subconscious intuition and conscious intellect as to what is felt and what is thought. If you indulge your feelings you are intuitive. When you use intuition to create a portrait, your confidence remains strong.

One of the mysteries of life is intuition. To debate intuition only intellectualizes the process and serves no purpose.

But intuition isn't without error. When using intuition, your exaggerated hopes and fears must not interfere. If you manipulate your intuitive thoughts, intuition becomes just wishful thinking. Intuition must develop spontaneously as a way of "just knowing."

Intuition works best when your brain is relaxed. Your self-knowledge comes in flashes of sudden insights. Many times you don't trust intuition because intuition isn't always clear. Intuition tells you if something is good in itself and/or that something is better or worse than something else.

When a problem in portraiture develops, your mind is doubtful. Intuition then solves the problem by filling in what is missing as your subconscious presents a new idea.

Trust the validity of intuition because most successful persons trust their intuition, although many aspects of intuition aren't explainable.

Exercise 8

For a few weeks or months record in a notebook every intuitive thought and the circumstances surrounding the thought. Note the first thought and when finished, concentrate on the first few seconds of that thought. The first few seconds are the most spontaneous and promising because the danger of rationalizing hasn't presented itself. Record the outcome of each intuitive thought. A pattern develops such as when you experience emotion with the intuitive insight, where the intuitive experience occurs, and the times the intuitive insight proves right or wrong.

Practicing this exercise brings patterns that stimulate your intuition. From these patterns of vague feelings, you develop confidence in your intuition.

Exercise 9

To become more aware of how intuition contributes to portraiture:
   • Practice guessing what might happen in a familiar situation.
   • Look at yourself in a mirror. Smile inwardly and notice how the face muscles subtly change. Frown inwardly and notice how the face muscles subtly change. By looking at your face muscles this way, you become more aware of how you actually feel.

Observation

To observe is to scan with the eye in order to store and/or record visual information. For portraiture, this means to just notice the total.

After you have learned to see the details of a portrait there is a tendency to become too involved with the minutiae of details. Now observation simplifies with a direct approach by seeing the overall portrait as if a spectator.

Exercise 10

To heighten your observation hold a portrait to a mirror to see the total portrait. Your varying viewpoint may reveal a total portrait which is pleasing or awkward to the eye.

Imagination

Imagination is the creation of an image from nothingness and having this process produce a mental image of pictures and/or words that aren't actually present in reality. In this respect, imagination is the true basis for creation.

Day dreaming, which is considered child's play, begins with imagined images, but as a child's play matures, language and organization add to the images. These additional elements enable the eye to see the finer points.

Creative imagery exists in disorder, but order develops as you select and interpret the events. Some guess work is involved as to whether your imagery is of major or minor importance.

Imagination deserves trust and is allowed to perform its functions of hopes, dreams, and anticipation. These functions keep imagination busy and prevent boredom. Your active, positive mind isn't restless, but secure and confident because your mind has little time for irritating and defeating thoughts.

To work with imagination means to look, see, observe, and interpret events with a degree of intuition. You are a person experiencing life and striving to bring experiences into articulate expression. Your experiences continue changing, so there is truly no one "permanent" image.

Exercise 11

Imagination, like anything else, improves if practiced. To conduct this exercise you should be in a relaxed environment with a relaxed mental and physical state, preferably with closed eyes.
   • Imagine an empty room.
   • Imagine the room with one person in outline form.
   • Imagine a complex person in the room with facial features and emotions such as smiling and laughing.
   • Imagine more than one person in the empty room.
   • Imagine the number of persons expands until the room is full.
   • Imagine the persons leave the room one by one until the room is empty.
In a similar exercise, use the ocean or sky as the complete background because the scale is liberated.

Exercise 12

A good way to activate the imagination is to take a field trip to your back yard or neighborhood. Look, see, and observe the mood and atmosphere with no purpose or commitment to make a portrait. With no pressures, your imagination is free to roam. Even if you don't make any portraits, you are activating your imagination with these experiences.

Anticipation

Anticipation is to expect, plan, and look forward to something and can produce a sense of enjoyment. The art of anticipation is related to the art of seeing.

The imagination triggers your anticipation which in turn stimulates and becomes valuable to expand your ability to see the "decisive moment" or the climax a fraction of a second before the decisive moment occurs. You learn to anticipate by acting beforehand. You prepare for a facial expression that is expected and you know the moment is probable. In reality, the true "decisive moment" comes after anticipation allows seeing and before the "decisive moment." This fraction of a second gives you time to capture the height of a person's expression.

Adding to anticipation is spontaneity. Your spontaneous action that should come in an effortless manner, is a result of a free and natural spirit requiring minimum thought. Spontaneity is lost if you act self-consciously by your inability to decide, plan, or act.

Anticipate if you make ten portraits and two are inferior, your average is 80 percent quality portraits.

Exercise 13

Anticipate other people's actions or ideas. You may be right or wrong, but you are anticipating.

Expression

To express is to translate an idea into a form such as a portrait. The central requirements of expression are a unifying force, theme, or focus which is obtained from repetition, contrast, and continuity. Artistically, expression means the ability to abstract, sort out, and separate the parts from the whole.

Exercise 14

Write an essay about a portrait. Writing is an act of learning and puts meaning on paper.

When you begin writing, you start with certain obvious goals, but you may turn an unexpected corner, be forced to see further, have a series of discoveries, and alter your direction.

Any time you combine writing, reading, and thinking the result is better than if the three are treated separately.

Exercise 15

Draw a sketch of the proposed portrait with no captions. Drawing improves thinking by adding eye-to-hand skills. Turn the sketch upside down to see the lines of design such as heavy, quick, and curved lines. Never fear, there is no right answer to this exercise.

Exercise 16

Write a description of a full length portrait of a person of any age. Cover the face in the portrait and write about what is remaining. Cover the body and write about what is remaining.

When only the body is observed, you see things as what kind of person belongs in the body such as an aristocrat or laborer. When only the face is observed, characteristics belonging to that particular person are seen.

Use words to describe your subject such as prim, mischievous, sophisticated, glamorous, sultry, mysterious, happy, pert, aloof, or wholesome. Some words group easily, while others counterpoint.

As you write, leave some sentences unfinished, to be completed later by someone else. The unfinished sentences create negative space, but when completed by others to become positive space, you will receive another viewpoint. Try it.

Exercise 17

Begin a collection of photographic portraits from posters, magazines, and prints.

Collecting begins by collecting everything. As you continue, there will be fewer portraits because your viewer's eye becomes more refined and selective. As quality replaces quantity, your collecting eventually demands that you turn your general collection of portraits into a specific collection. You may want to add to your visual sensitivity by collecting only certain categories such as portraits of men, children, women, portraits made by women or Europeans, or of a certain era.

THE CREATIVE PROCESS

Defining the Creative Process

To create is the building block bringing into existence something that has its own identity. A creation is born by nurturing a series of skillful, imaginative thoughts and actions. In this process, creative skill and imagination increase from personal experiences, the study of history, refinement of technique, and the interaction with culture in the way you live.

Creativity turns form into art which develops sensitivities and encourages orientation to beauty. Whether plain or elaborate, beauty is meaningful and pleasing.

The Birth of Creativity

Creativity arrives as flashes in the mind that is open to ideas. These initial flashes of nervous excitement in the brain represent the imagination producing a new idea. Action must be taken on the imagination or an idea has no value. Acting on any specific idea serves to breed another idea that is often better. These related ideas eventually fuse into a stable union.

Creativity associates with free thought, dreams, and imagination to exist in the realm of the subconscious brought forward. Creativity thrives best when paired with relaxation because a relaxed state receives new arousals and ideas with greater ease. You, the creator, now act only as a spectator to the content flashing through your mind.

Creativity is enhanced when you make no commitment to any initial thoughts, but take time to evaluate the new thoughts with other thoughts already in your mind's storage system. The ideas come from simple everyday living experiences that demand attention and rarely arrive from complicated so-called formulas or theories. Delaying any action isn't procrastination, but a stretching and enlightening time. The ultimate goal is to work the ideas to create order.

In the second phase of creativity, the initial idea is translated into reality. These second thoughts relate to logic and analysis. This second thought process makes the "inside" forces visible and involves a much greater time period that may consume days, even years. Without the second thought phase, ideas from the initial thoughts are unnoticed or, if noticed, appear only as enthusiasm. The blast of initial thoughts fuels the difficult work of second thoughts when acted upon, and shows initiative and practical results.

The second thoughts in creativeness give your initial thoughts their control, direction, and professionalism. Any creative endeavor is governed by your knowledge and skill, whether natural or acquired. Art forms require ten-percent craft, ninety-percent thinking.

Portraiture, similar to most other art forms, has two sides—technical and creative. Stimulation in the brain prompts you to use the technical knowledge of portraiture to become a participant in your work. At this point you create what you like or prefer.

At the same time, you must balance your ego to create. A strong ego is required for you to feel you are the only individual creating a unique work of art. Yet, you must set aside your ego to allow yourself to grow.

Nurturing Creativity

The creative instinct within you is a positive, constructive force handled several ways. You recognize creativity in yourself, and continually produce and nurture thoughts and actions from your creative mind. Or you can allow creativity to lie stagnant for years only to later develop your awareness and potential. Usually, where there are interests, thoughts, and actions, however latent, there is talent.

Instinct, an aspect of creativity, comes from a natural aptitude inherited at birth in varying proportions. Every person possesses instinct, although it can be stunted by ignoring the artistic side of life and by minimum exposure to art.

People are born with sense organs that respond to seeing, hearing, smelling, tasting, and touching. Each of these five senses are proportioned, or allocated, at birth. These proportions provide different abilities such as musical, athletic, and artistic. Senses can't be taught, but they can be nourished. The inherited elements combine with living experiences and develop into the creation of chosen art forms.

Creativity is best nourished by not discouraging or destroying your desire to create. This sounds ludicrous, but nothing destroys creativity more than negative influences or tendencies. Nourishing creativity promotes growth.

Nurture creativity by defining and encouraging the positive aspects of your creative effort.

Nurture creativity with your time. Creativity demands time and concentration to form thoughts.

Nurture creativity by placing yourself in your preferred situation. If you perform best by working on a project until it is solidified, and then make a commitment which brings pressure, this procedure is okay. If you work best by making a commitment first, by signing a contract or making a sale, this approach is also okay.

Nurture creativity by priming yourself with other people's art. Nothing starts the creative juices flowing more than to see, admire, and emulate other art with your style.

Nurture creativity further by your writing in a journal. Record thoughts that come from every aspect of your thinking.

Nurture creativity by developing a retrieval system for your collection of ideas. Nothing frustrates you more than to have an earlier idea set aside and then not be able to locate it when needed.

Nurture creativity by acknowledging and appreciating the need for your art. Nothing stalls creativity more than assuming that your art is purposeless.

Characteristics of Creative Persons

Not everyone possesses all the common characteristics of a creative individual, but one common denominator enjoyed by most creative persons is that they process those initial and second imaginative thoughts, that I discussed earlier, differently from the masses.

Although creativity stems from nonconformist thinking, creative persons share certain common characteristics. Nonconformist thinking comes to those who deviate from the "accepted" path.

Conformists follow the path. Those who conform are easily recognizable and the nonconformist blazing new paths is sometimes difficult to identify as being creative. But conformity balances the nonconforming creative process because conformity allows society as a whole to function smoothly while the nonconforming individual seeks and finds new paths that the conformist later follows.

Creative persons see beauty in everything such as subject, shape, form, color, and texture. The most mundane scene can hold beauty.

Creative persons are involved with a force that allows creativity just for its own sake.

Creative persons possess and balance opposite tensions: intellect versus intuition, conscious versus subconscious, conforming versus nonconforming, and simple versus complex.

Creative persons amplify any stimuli because they are always stretching their imagination with their experiences.

Creative persons listen carefully to vague feelings that are not yet fully developed.

Creative persons aren't disturbed by chaos, imbalance, and counterpoint. Symmetry is good, but asymmetry is a challenge to order.

Creative persons reach deeper, broader, and more flexibly into their awareness of themselves and others.

Creative persons are interested in the potential rather than faulting the solution. An initial imaginative idea is a potential solution and a legitimate reason for further elaboration. The second imaginative thought which involves actual creation presents a new way to create.

Creative persons display openness, independence, and confidence because to transform a feeling into a form is not frightening.

Creative persons aren't afraid of laughing at themselves or afraid of others laughing at them.

Creative persons don't shy away from the hard work of creativity. Toughness, resiliency, and renewal evolve from being creative.

Creative persons aren't afraid of the demand placed on them by others or themselves.

Creative persons aren't afraid to participate in a learning process.

Creative persons respond spontaneously to problems as a form of creativity. Creative persons form their own questions, find the answers, and activate changes.

Creative persons recognize luck as an integral part of creativity. They see the "accidents" that occur in their lives as luck.

Creative persons respond to their work seriously, yet

discover their most serious work is play that refreshes, stimulates, and inspires.

Creative persons are alert to the possibilities of isolation. Often they function best when left alone with their ideas.

Creative persons demand control over their work.

Creative persons are leery of comfortable ruts. The risk of novelty and new paths offers flexibility and requires working at the outer edge of their ability.

Creative persons function better the more critical they become of their work, and consider their criticism as progress.

Creative persons aren't afraid to share their creative problems because when they explain the problem to others, they clarify and see the problem from another viewpoint.

Creative persons immerse themselves in their area of interest, permit the ideas to mature, and enjoy the results.

Creative persons know that the true source of creativity lies in guidelines, structure, and rules because too much unbridled freedom imprisons the mind.

Exercise

The best exercise is to make a portrait. Studying creativity does not substitute for the actual creating. There is an excitement in making a portrait which stimulates the imagination and radiates enthusiasm to make the next portrait.

·-FOUR-·

"LINES OF DESIGN"

Defining Lines of Design

Lines of design are the elements of a portrait that form a real or illusionary pattern which the viewer's eye can follow. These major and minor patterns form expressive shapes and movement with linear elements, texture, color, and light and dark values.

The lines of design for portraiture are arranged for the three-dimensional effect, emotional dimension, and use of color.

Lines of Design for Three Dimensions

The lines of design when properly composed and used as building blocks transform a two-dimensional flat surface portrait into a surface with an illusion of three dimensions.

Length (the distance from side to side) and width (the distance from top to bottom) are always present. Depth creates the distance from front to back and is not actually present, but is visually created with lines of design.

Exercise 1

The camera lens doesn't add depth perception because the camera lens has only one "eye." An approach to envision what the camera lens sees is shown in Figure 4-1. Raise one hand to shoulder height with your elbow straight. In this hand hold vertically a small bottle with about a one inch opening. Raise the other hand to above shoulder height with your elbow bent slightly. Hold a pencil vertically in this hand. Close one eye and try to place the pencil in the bottle opening. You'll find that it's difficult to determine how far the bottle is from you with only one eye open because there is no depth perception. Now, open both eyes and see how easy you put the pencil in the bottle with depth perception.

Depth perception can be created on two-dimensional surfaces by lines of design such as linear perspective, aerial perspective, overlap, placement, detail, size gradation, transparency, light, shadow, and color.

Linear Perspective

Linear perspective involves the mechanics of extended lines. Parallel lines that recede to the distant background appear to converge inside the format at an imaginary point called the vanishing point, Figure 4-2. The lines carry the viewer's eye into deep space quickly or slowly, depending on how you arrange the lines.

If the linear perspective is exaggerated, the lines converge at a point outside of the format, Figure 4-3, and lead the viewer's eye out of the portrait.

Aerial Perspective

Aerial perspective is the use of color and/or light and dark to create imaginary depth. Aerial perspective generally follows linear perspective because objects seen in the distance appear less clear and less sharp than the nearer objects. The quality of the atmosphere makes the distant objects appear muted in color, bluer and grayer, and with softened outlines and forms that often blend into one another.

Overlap

Overlap creates the illusion of deep space by causing the object closest to the viewer to hide part of the next closest object. This series continues until there are no more objects. The closest object actually stands in front of another to subtract part of the farthest object. The size of the objects doesn't matter because once an overlap is made, the viewer assumes the overlapping object is closest. The spatial relationship is formed from a front to back sequence, or the sequence is reversed. The overlapping objects unite to become one larger unit.

The objects are further distinguished if they appear in light and dark values. One arrangement is black in the back, gray in the middle, and white in the front. For a more dramatic effect the reverse arrangement is white in the back, gray in the middle, and black in the front.

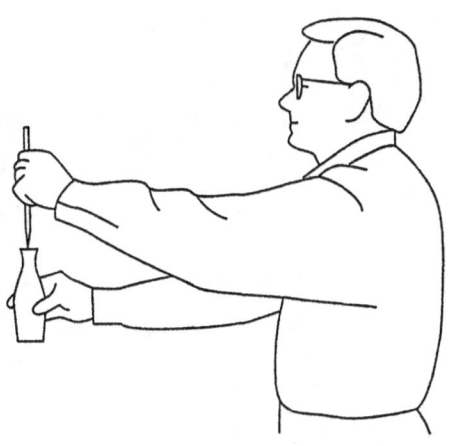

Figure 4-1
Depth Perception

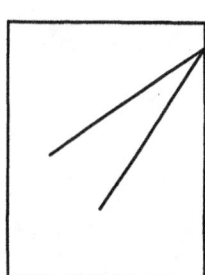

Figure 4-2
Vanishing Point Lines Converge
Inside Format

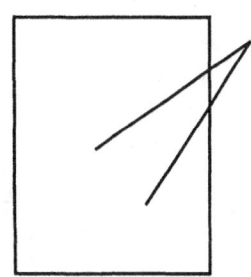

Figure 4-3
Vanishing Point Lines Converge
Outside Format

Placement

The placement of the lines of design establishes three dimensions and emphasis. Placement assumes that the horizon line appears at eye level. The viewer judges the area above the horizon line farther away than the area below the horizon line. In the area below the horizon line, the closer the object is to the bottom of the format, the closer the object appears. In the area above the horizon line, the farther the object is from the horizon line, the farther the object appears.

Detail

The viewer's eye doesn't simultaneously see clearly and in great detail the near and far objects. If the near objects look sharp, the farther objects look unfocused. Foreground is associated with sharpness and background with haziness and less detail.

Size Gradation

Size gradation is change in an orderly manner. Gradation generates an optical illusion and progresses to a climax. In size gradation different sizes progress from small to large or large to small. The gradation is in a straight or curved path.

Transparency

Anything transparent is "seen through." Transparency doesn't stop the viewer's eye; there is no complete "covering up" of an object because the contour of the object remains entirely visible and the covered-up object doesn't cease to exist. Transparent objects are seen simultaneously when superimposed on each other, rather than lined edge to edge. Transparency negates overlap, so both shapes—the closest and farthest—are allowed to show.

Light and Shadow

Light and shadow express depth. If there isn't a shadow there is no depth; if there is some shadow, there is some depth; and if there is a large amount of shadow there is a large amount of depth.

A good shadow created by a single light source gives strong definition to the third dimension and separates the subject from the background. The variation of the shadow's thickness further separates.

Shadow gives information about an object. The position of an object is determined by its shadow.

A shadow cuts into an object to question the continuity of that object.

A shadow creates its own profile or contour resulting in an object itself. A shadow is less permanent in feeling than the actual object.

Color

Every color that the eyes perceive produces a universal, direct, and immediate response. Everyone has definite color preferences. Harmonious or contrasting color rhythms are acceptable if they satisfy aesthetic values. Colors that don't satisfy are rejected.

Color is integrated into a portrait by being used in a direct manner to model the various spatial planes of the two-dimensional surface. This is accomplished by using certain combinations of colors in a system of well-ordered color relationships.

Color pertaining to its definition, characteristics, nature, color schemes by relationships and percentages, and enhancing the use of color is discussed on pages 56-62, 132-134. See Using Color for Portraiture on the back cover.

Lines of Design for Emotional Dimension

The lines of design for emotion form the "words" of the "story" in the composition and express your feelings. Bad composition is merely a bad choice of the lines of design.

The lines of design produce and control the unseen and suggest movement by what the memory associates with them such as the S curve associates with femininity and the straight line with masculinity.

The viewer's eye traveling over the path created by the lines of design has a difficult or easy time depending on the way the viewer is accustomed to reading the written word—from left to right, right to left, or up and down. The visual image, unlike the written word, is read in jumps with long or short pauses and backtracking to various lines of design. Therefore, the lines of design need to help the viewer.

Your lines of design in a portrait introduce a line of any duration creating movement through space which results in space on either side. For example, a prop such as a fence post creates a vertical line with space on each side which can have degrees of light and dark on either side.

A line cutting through space creates shape. An actual line shows contour while an imaginary line shows transition.

An actual or illusionary line, however small, has certain characteristics such as measurement, type, direction, location, and character.

A line's measurement is the length, width, and depth which unites or divides the portrait. If a line is thin, the ends aren't as important as a line that is broad. The ends (such as pointed, square, or round) can continue or stop the line.

A line's type is the general appearance such as straight, curved, diagonal, or zigzag. The straight line, repetitious; the curve, graceful; the diagonal, abrupt; the zigzag, jagged.

The direction of the line is vertical, horizontal, or diagonal, and gives continuity.

The character of a line is identified by the edge, such as soft or hard. A soft line shows tranquility. A heavy, hard line shows excitement and drama. A significant edge is light or dark. These lines are forms of blank space or occupied space. Forms occupying space are called positive spaces. Blank space around occupied or positive space, is called negative space.

The lines, when closed, give shape such as a square, rectangle, triangle, circle, and oval. When these two-dimensional shapes are side lighted, the shape has three-dimensional form.

Originating Line

The originating line of all lines of design is a mark known as a dot which serves as a separate entity or as the first of a following line that instructs the viewer. As a separate entity, if the small mark is regular-shaped, no movement is shown. If the small mark is irregular-shaped, some movement is shown, Figure 4-4.

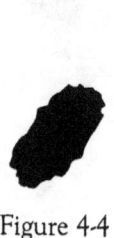

Figure 4-4
Dot

Straight Lines

Straight Line

The straight line is a dot extended horizontally, vertically, or diagonally, Figure 4-5. The straight line is easy to read because there is no interference. Its simplicity prepares the viewer's eye for a possible curve or angle. A straight line suggests masculinity, strength, and man-made.

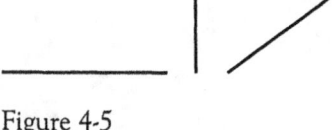

Figure 4-5
Straight Line

Horizontal Line

The horizontal line, Figure 4-6, suggests repose, passiveness, peace, quiet, calm, rest, relaxation, finality, and stability. The varied horizontal line avoids monotony and is more casual than a vertical line.

Figure 4-6
Horizontal Line

Vertical Line

The vertical line, Figure 4-7, suggests height, pride, dignity, stability, strength, forthrightness, power, and stature. Vertical lines represent nobility as in people. Vertical lines create tension because a vertical line requires a balancing effort to stand erect. The vertical line is more formal than the horizontal line and easy to read because of few interferences.

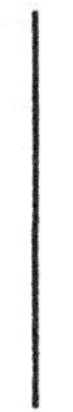

Figure 4-7
Vertical Line

Long Vertical Line

The long vertical line, Figure 4-8, shows dignity and melancholy.

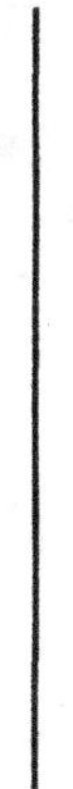

Short Vertical Line

The short vertical line, Figure 4-9, shows less loftiness than the long line. The short line placed next to a long line dramatizes the longer line.

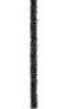

Figure 4-8
Long Vertical Line

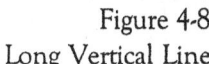

Figure 4-9
Short Vertical Line

"L" Shape

Within the straight line is the "L" shape, Figure 4-10 which suggests informality and flexibility by moving left or right.

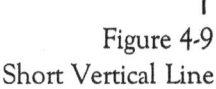

Figure 4-10
"L" Shape

Cross

The cross shape, Figure 4-11, suggests unity and awe.

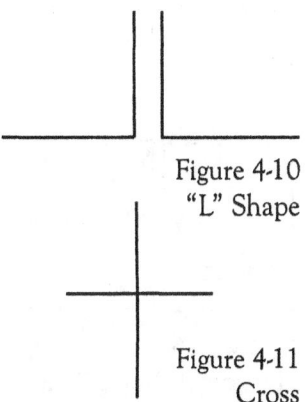

Figure 4-11
Cross

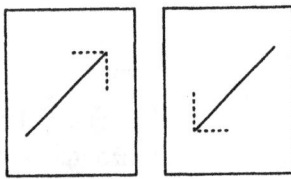

Figure 4-12
Ascending and Descending
Vertical Lines

Ascending and Descending Vertical Lines
 Ascending vertical lines suggest freedom from weight while descending vertical lines suggest drama, Figure 4-12.

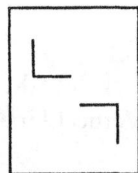

Figure 4-13
Balanced Vertical and
Horizontal Lines

Balanced Vertical and Horizontal Lines
 Perfectly balanced vertical and horizontal lines void any sense of movement, Figure 4-13.

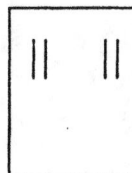

Figure 4-14
Vertical Lines Near Top of
Format

Vertical Lines Near Top of Format
 The closer the vertical lines are placed to the top of the format, the loftier the subject appears, Figure 4-14.

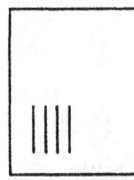

Figure 4-15
Vertical Parallel Lines

Vertical Parallel Lines
 Vertical parallel lines suggest energy, Figure 4-15.

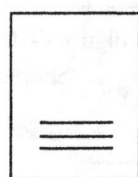

Figure 4-16
Horizontal Parallel Lines

Horizontal Parallel Lines
 Horizontal parallel lines suggest rest, Figure 4-16.

Diagonal Lines

Diagonal lines show dynamic action, movement, continuity, excitement, imbalance, instability, falling, a receding into the background, force, and rising and falling with dynamics, Figure 4-17.

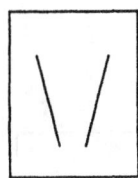

Figure 4-17
Diagonal Lines

Rows of Diagonal Lines

Rows of diagonal lines show procession and progression, Figure 4-18.

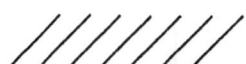

Figure 4-18
Rows of Diagonal Lines

Diagonal Line Extends to Edge

The diagonal line loses its movement when the line extends to the edge of the format, Figure 4-19.

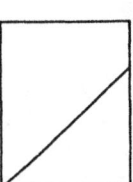

Figure 4-19
Diagonal Line Extends to Edge

Diagonal Line Extends from One Corner to Opposite Corner

The effect is static if the diagonal line extends from one corner to the opposite corner of the format, Figure 4-20.

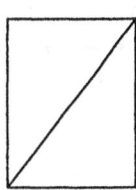

Figure 4-20
Diagonal Line Extends from
One Corner to Opposite Corner

Zigzag Lines

Zigzag lines or conflicting diagonals are a series of short, long, straight, or curved lines that as they turn connect smoothly or sharply, Figure 4-21. The zigzag lines according to the turns create a path such as abrupt, smooth, animation, feminine, and masculine.

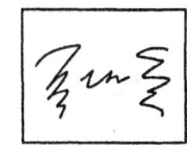

Figure 4-21
Zigzag Lines

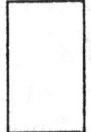

Figure 4-22
Square

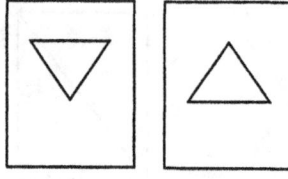

Figure 4-23
Rectangle

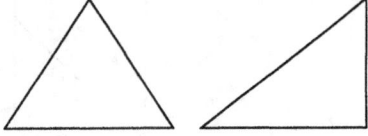

Figure 4-24
Triangle

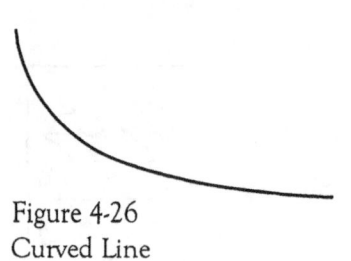

Figure 4-25
Pyramid

Straight Lines Joined

  Straight lines when joined at angles form a square, rectangle, triangle, and pyramid.

Square

  A square, Figure 4-22, having four equal sides and four 90 degree angles can't vary in any one dimension and still be a square. Squareness equates to being static.

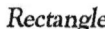

Rectangle

  A rectangle is a flat figure with adjacent sides of unequal length and four 90 degree angles, Figure 4-23. Rectangles show movement.

Triangle

  A triangle has three sides and three angles to exemplify the pointed shape. The triangle that is equilateral is stable and represents spiritedness, Figure 4-24. The irregular shape triangle denotes movement.

Pyramid

  A pyramid shape has a broad supporting base narrowing gradually to a point. The pyramid shape exerts permanence, stability, keenness, endurance, and alertness. The upside down pyramid conveys inferiority, lightness, and weakness, Figure 4-25.

Curved Lines

Curved Line

  The curved line is a straight line under tension. The curve, pleasing to the viewer's eye, conveys motion, gracefulness, energy, growth, femininity, slowness, meandering beauty, charm, restfulness, and delicacy. The sharper the curve, the more suggestion of action, gaiety, and excitement, Figure 4-26.

Figure 4-26
Curved Line

S Curve Line Read Left to Right

The S curve line is read left to right quickly and with ease, Figure 4-27.

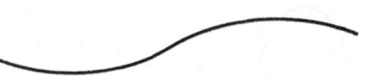

Figure 4-27
S Curve Line Read Left to Right

S Curve Line Read Right to Left

The S curve line is read right to left, slowly and with "tragic" qualities, Figure 4-28.

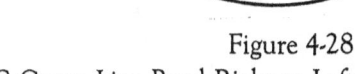

Figure 4-28
S Curve Line Read Right to Left

Curved line movement includes a spiral, circle, oval, dome, Gothic Arch, Roman Arch, grief line, and youth or happy line.

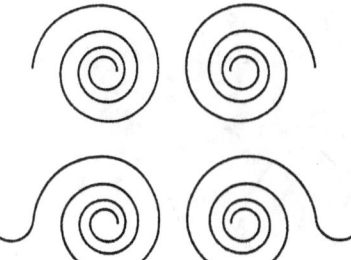

Figure 4-29
Spiral

Spiral

The spiral is a line circling another center point, Figure 4-29. It moves left to right or right to left and indicates a diversion from the conforming path. At the free end the spiral can have a counterpoint movement or an abrupt end.

Circle

A circle is a closed plane with every point equally distant from a fixed center point. The circle has no angles, is continuous, powerful, compact, nondirectional, and holds your attention, Figure 4-30.

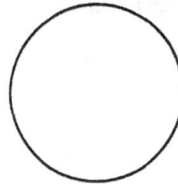

Figure 4-30
Circle

Oval

The oval is an ellipsoidal shape and suggests serenity with movement, Figure 4-31.

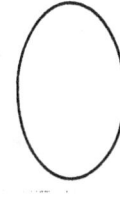

Figure 4-31
Oval

Dome

The dome is an elliptical shape which uplifts and is buoyant, Figure 4-32.

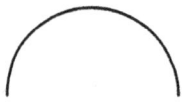

Figure 4-32
Dome

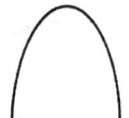

Figure 4-33
Gothic Arch

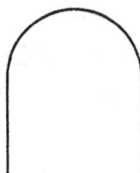

Figure 4-34
Roman Arch

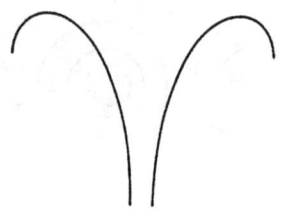

Figure 4-35
Grief Line

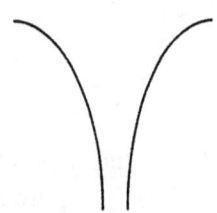

Figure 4-36
Youth or Happy Line

Gothic Arch

The Gothic Arch is a pointed arch and symbolizes contemplation and aspiration to higher ideals. It's best portrayed with long, thin vertical lines reaching a curved point, Figure 4-33.

Roman Arch

The Roman Arch, the opposite of the Gothic Arch, is a semi-circular arch with lines that adhere to the ground. It conveys support, weight, and solemnness, Figure 4-34.

Grief Line

The grief line is a modified Roman Arch with the shortening of the line following the curve. It infers tragedy and melancholy, Figure 4-35.

Youth or Happy Line

The youth or happy line is a Roman Arch further modified by additional shortening of the line following the curve. The youth or happy line conveys happiness and liveliness, Figure 4-36. This additional shortening of the curve by only a fraction demonstrates the fine line between laughter and tears.

Lines of Design for Color

Defining Color

Sir Isaac Newton in the seventeenth century discovered that color is a property of light, not a separate entity, as he passed a beam of sunlight or white light through a glass prism, Figure 4-37. As the light passed through the prism a rainbow of colors formed called a spectrum. The major hues or colors were easily distinguishable as red, orange, yellow, green, blue, indigo, and violet. These colors are shown within the twelve-color Color

Wheel. See Using Color for Portraiture on the back cover: Part I, Color Wheel. The Color Wheel has the same progression of colors as the spectrum but is bent into a circle. The two end colors are blended into red-violet which is a color not present in the spectrum.

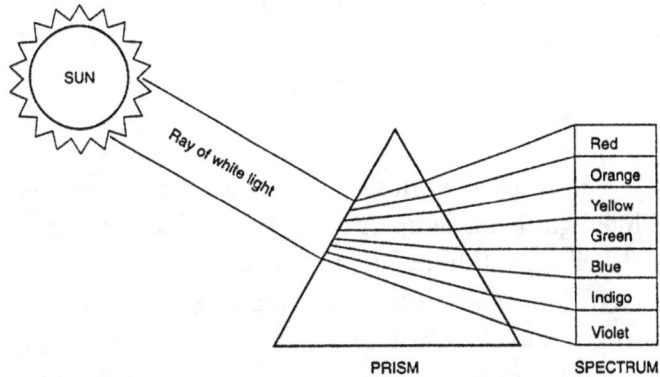

Figure 4-37
Source of Color

The light from each color has different wave lengths. Reading from the longest and strongest to the shortest and weakest is red, orange, yellow, green, blue, indigo, and violet. The viewer's eye receives a slightly different sensation from each wave length permitting the brain to recognize various colors.

To further define color I've presented a series of color wheels and charts on the back cover to coordinate with the following discussions of the characteristics of color, nature of color, and color schemes. See Using Color for Portraiture on the back cover.

Characteristics of Color

The characteristics of color: hue, value, and intensity. See Using Color for Portraiture on the back cover: Part I, Hues on the Color Wheel; Part II, Value Scale; and Part III, Intensity Scale.

Hue is the common name of the color such as red, blue, or green. Hue designates the color's position on the color wheel and is changed only by being mixed with another color. No black or white is added. When three or four neighboring hues on the color wheel contain one common color which dominates, these colors are analogous or alike. A color that is mixed from a hue and black is called a shade such as deep brown. A color that is made with a hue and white is a tint such as pink and ivory. A color that is made of a hue, black, and white is a tone such as tan. Hue indicates the color's temperature such as warm or cool.

Value defines the lightness or darkness of the hue due to the quantity of light reflected or transmitted from it. Value is created by adding the neutrals, white or black, and as a result, there are many steps of values between the lightest and darkest hue.

Intensity defines the purity, strength, richness, or saturation of a color derived from the quality of light. Intensity distinguishes a brighter tone of a color from a duller tone of the same hue. Changes of intensity are made by adding a neutral of white, gray, or black or by adding any of the complimentary colors.

Nature of Color

Most people can see in the spectrum six or seven colors. But white light is made up of three basic colors: the primary colors of red, yellow, and blue. The secondary colors are green, orange, and violet. The triadic colors are yellow-green, blue-violet, and red-orange. All colors can be produced by a selective mixture of the three primary colors. See Using Color for Portraiture on the back cover: Part I, Color Wheel.

Colors have a "mind temperature" bringing advancing and receding effects and are enjoyed without awareness. The advancing colors of red, yellow, and orange are associated with the color of the sun and heat, and are "warm" colors. Warm colors excite, stimulate, and appear closer. The receding colors of blue and green are associated with colors of the water, sky, and vegetation, and are "cool" colors. Cool colors relax, recede, and appear farther.

The characteristics of the primary colors:

Red

Red is advancing, warm, dynamic, aggressive, active, strong, positive, stimulating, radiant, and erotic. Red means danger, violence, virility, temper, and revolution. The colors of flames and blood are associated with red. If red is set against white or a light colored background, the radiance appears dim and dull. If red is set against black or a dark colored background, a fiery power exists.

Yellow

Yellow is the lightest and brightest of all pure colors. It's advancing, pleasant, neutral, uplifting, sunny, bright, spring-like, and cheery. Yellow negatively means cowardliness and sickness. Yellow is the color nearest to white. If yellow stands against white, warmth and depth are shown.

Blue

Blue is receding, cold, passive, restful, tranquil, restrained, emits a feeling of depression, and shows a lack of excitement. Blue is associated with the sky and is used as background. Blue isn't very sensitive to changes; for example, a mixture of blue can be varied a couple of steps on either side and remain a pure color.

The characteristics of the secondary colors:

Green

Green is restful, tranquil, cheerful, versatile, open, genuine, quiet, soothing, and slightly cool. Green is not a dull neutral, doesn't advance or recede, and is neither hot or cold. Green is associated with growth. Green, when seen by reflected light, appears darker. Green, when seen against the light, appears brighter and more luminous.

Orange

Orange combines the brilliance of yellow and the warmth of red to be advancing, warm, and luminous. Its warmth is not as prominent as red. Halloween, Thanksgiving, and Autumn are associated with orange.

Violet

Violet combines red and blue and is directly opposite yellow on the color wheel and ranges from pale lavender to black-purple. Pure violet, made of one-half red and one-half blue, is the darkest of color hues. In its deeper tones, violet infers sophistication, daringness, and death. If violet contains lots of red, it's active and denotes royalty. If violet contains lots of blue, it's passive and cold.

White, gray, and black are neutrals and do not look like any color on the spectrum. From a scientific standpoint the neutrals reflect all of the color rays of light. The neutrals are affected by the quantity of light reflected, whereas color relates to the quality of light reflected.

The characteristics of the neutrals:

White

White is free from color, shows the most energy, dazzles the eye, and the brightest of all. White is associated with health and cleanliness.

The viewer's eye travels first to white. White makes most brilliant colors seem less bright, and can't be influenced by other colors.

White enlarges the area in which it exists. Off-white adapts as a better decorative color. If a white sheer fabric rests next to the skin, the skin tone shows through. A portrait dominated by white appears cool.

Gray

Gray is produced from a blending of white and black. It's expressionless, mysterious, ambiguous, cool, puzzling, receding, and the most neutral of colors. Dark gray is conventional. Light gray is innocent, sensitive, and subtle. Gray is associated with overcast skies, conservative businesses, and sickness. The environment gives gray vitality and weakens any luminosity of the same environment.

Black

Black is hueless, sophisticated, and associated with night. Black functions primarily to set off colors at their maximum luminosity. Black directs the viewer's eye to a focal point. Black is influenced by surrounding colors, such as black adjacent to green takes on a greenish cast.

Exercise 2

To aid in using the lines of design for color three exercises with combined results can be preformed:
• Through the viewfinder rack the camera out of focus to lose the detail. See how easily you locate the light and dark areas which form the lines of design.
• Squint your eyes almost closed to assimilate an "f/22" aperture opening. This viewpoint eliminates detail, permits you to see "impressionistically," and the overall brightness diminishes so that you distinguish color contrasts. This frees the colors from the subject matter.
• To isolate the lines of design, form a rectangle or square format with your thumbs and index fingers, Figure 4-38. Then look through the format to eliminate color lines of design outside your format.

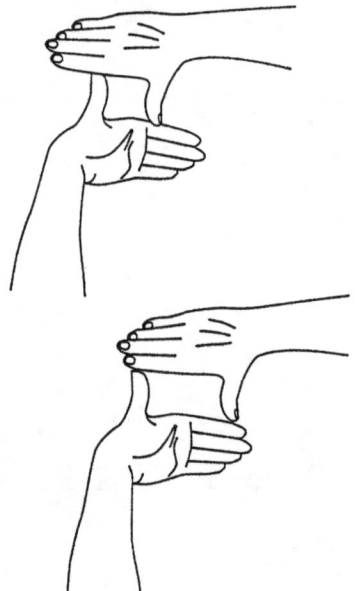

Figure 4-38
Square and Rectangle Formats
Formed With Hands

Selection of Portrait Color Scheme by Relationships

Every color is obsessed with being the center of attention. Using color depends on your understanding of color relationships. A color used singularly only has its own characteristics. When a single color appears with another color or several other colors the magic of color occurs as the single color changes itself and the neighboring colors.

An overall color scheme for a portrait can be monochromatic, analogous, complimentary, and triadic. See Using Color for Portraiture on the back cover: Part IV, Selection of Portrait Color Scheme by Relationships. Monochromatic uses one hue on the color wheel in varying shades of intensity to create drama. Analogous uses three colors adjoining each other on the color wheel and produces a quiet and passive effect. Complimentary or contrasting colors use colors that are directly opposite each other on the color wheel to create intensity, excitement, and show movement. The triadic color scheme is created from any three hues that are located equidistant from each other on the color wheel and creates restiveness.

Included in the color selection for a portrait is selecting the clothes color scheme by percentages which is discussed on pages 132-134.

Enhancing the Use Of Color

To enhance the use of color you must apply the major principles of rhythm, balance, center of interest, and proportion along with minor principles of repetition, alternation, progression, sequence, and contrast.

Rhythm

The selection of the colors forms movement which can repeat at intervals to form reoccurring climaxes.

Balance

To balance is to create a sense of equalness by numerical count, feeling, or worth. Balance can be formal or informal. Colors that are dark appear heavier than light colors. If not lighted a color looks dark. One way you create balance and unity is to repeat colors throughout the portrait.

Center of Interest

The center of interest is the dominant force. All elements lead the viewer's eye to this converging point.

Color schemes with equal parts of color don't receive as much attention as when one color dominates. The viewer's eye is confused when one color doesn't dominate or become the center of interest.

Proportion

Color proportion is balancing how the colors deal with each other in a ratio that is pleasing to the viewer's eye.

Introducing variety to keep from being monotonous requires one color to relate to another in factors such as size, tone, hue, and mass.

Repetition

Repetition is to use an object again and again to establish a pattern. Whatever the design, once repeated the intensity magnifies the object. Repetition is the simplest design system to use colors effectively and whether large or small creates immediate harmony. Repetition causes dominance of a visual object and rhythm.

Alternation

Alternation is to present objects or colors repeatedly by using one object or color, then switch to another object or color.

Progression

Progression is to move forward with improvement. After the viewer's eye focuses on the color at the center of interest, the eye moves forward to other color areas. The progression can be quick, slow, steady, or abrupt.

Sequence

Sequence is the order in which objects appear. Color leads easily to another color or is followed easily by another color. Reversely, colors lead and follow with difficulty.

Contrast

Contrast is difference. The large or small difference depends on the desired effect. The further apart the hue intervals, the stronger the contrast.

Selection of Color Film for a Portrait

Regardless of your use of the lines of design for color, your choice of color film has a significant effect on the outcome of your portrait.

There are two popular types of color film: color negative film, commonly called color print film; color positive film, commonly called color slide film. Each type is further categorized as daylight (from the sun) or tungsten (from artificial light).

The film for color print film has three main emulsion layers that are sensitive to red, green, and blue light. These three colors appear only at the end of the process. In between exposure and the final print, chemicals layered with the three colors bring forth the color dyes during the development for each layer. Yellow appears in the blue sensitive layer, magenta in the green sensitive layer, and cyan in the red sensitive layer. When viewing the color print negative the original three colors are altered, but corrected in the final printing. Color negative film has tolerance in exposure settings.

Color positive film prints the actual color as color slides. Color slide exposures need to be exact requiring a narrow exposure tolerance. If you are not sure of the exact exposure, then bracket your exposures which is the making of the same pose with one or more exposures that are overexposed and one or more exposures that are underexposed.

In choosing the appropriate color film, consideration is given to definition, sharpness, and graininess. Definition is the clarity of detail, sharpness determines whether the edges between light and dark are sharp, and graininess is when the grains of the film become larger to create a sand-pebble appearance.

Your choice of color film for a portrait depends on the results desired.

~ F I V E ~

COMPOSITION

Defining Composition

Composition is the bringing together of creative thoughts and actions into a form by assembling and arranging the parts to demonstrate "aliveness." Composition functions to keep the viewer's eye in the format, to lead the eye, and to coax the eye to various objects.

Composition, a matter of choice, provides the most vivid way to divide an area confined by four boundaries. "Art" has a strong tendency to slough off anything not involving free choices.

The composition gives a sequential flow of the elements on the two-dimensional surface to create an illusion. The more elements the more complex the portrait. A good approach is knowing what to omit. Often, by showing less, more is shown. There is a definite pleasure in omitting something.

The object of the lines of design in composition is the continuity of visual expression. The structure of these lines of design provide the discipline of arrangement.

When structure is rigid, closely followed, with balanced concentration of elements, the arrangement is formal. Semi-formal arrangements are rigid except for the concentration of less balanced elements. Informal arrangement is free with few guidelines. All lines, whether formal, semi-formal, or informal have actual or illusionary lines of design. The conformity to a line of design is broken by any irregularity or departure from the overall line of design. The effectiveness of the conformity is heightened when there is a purpose such as demanding attention, preventing monotony, or changing the regular structure.

Composition is basic to any portrait. Without composition, you become the innovator, creator, producer, and critic of the ordinary. You enjoy learning composition because the learning process furthers art in any form.

If you make a portrait showing aliveness without benefit of rules and guidelines, this is commendable. But if you can't intuitively make a portrait that evokes a stirring response, you benefit from knowing the composition rules and guidelines.

If you know the rules, you are free from indecision and uncertainty to break the rules when interpreting them. If you break the rules, you need to break them forcefully and freely.

Some critics say that if a beginner learns the rules, any natural ability is destroyed. But the harmonious integrity of balance and rhythm you use to compose a unique portrait can't be hampered regardless of the rules you learn. Harmony is instinctive and appears as a magic formula. In reality, you are the magic in the formula because of how you see.

A beginner benefits from adhering to guidelines. When you begin composing, you make decisions cautiously and slowly. As you learn more about composition, the principles of organization serve only as suggestions for seeing. Later, when you know the rules, you compose quickly because composing becomes second nature. As you become more knowledgeable of composition you see only what you are prepared to see.

Compositional Guidelines

Good composition has one focal point or center of interest. More than one center of interest creates divided attention for the viewer.

Composition exerts control as the viewer's eye always seeks the center of interest. The remaining space is filled because, if not, the viewer's eye sees nothing and wanders to the edge of the format seeking relief.

"Rule of Thirds"

One of the more traditional approaches of organizing the elements in a composition is the "Rule of Thirds" based on the traditional Greek "Golden Oblong" of a rectangle with an approximate 8 to 5 ratio, as shown in Figure 5-1.

In the Rule of Thirds the space, whether a rectangle, oval, circle, or square, is divided into three sections horizontally and vertically resulting in four intersecting points in the lower left, lower right, upper left, and upper right, Figure 5-2. The viewer's eye rests in the general area of the four intersecting points.

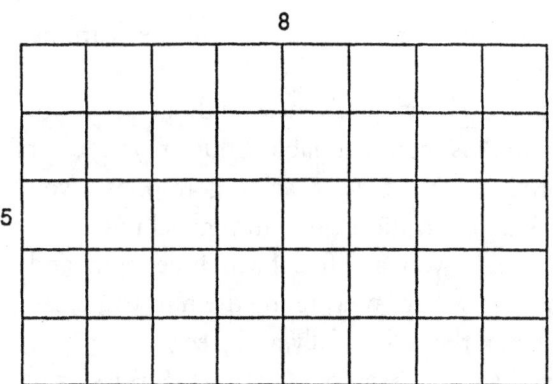

Figure 5-1
"Rule of Thirds"

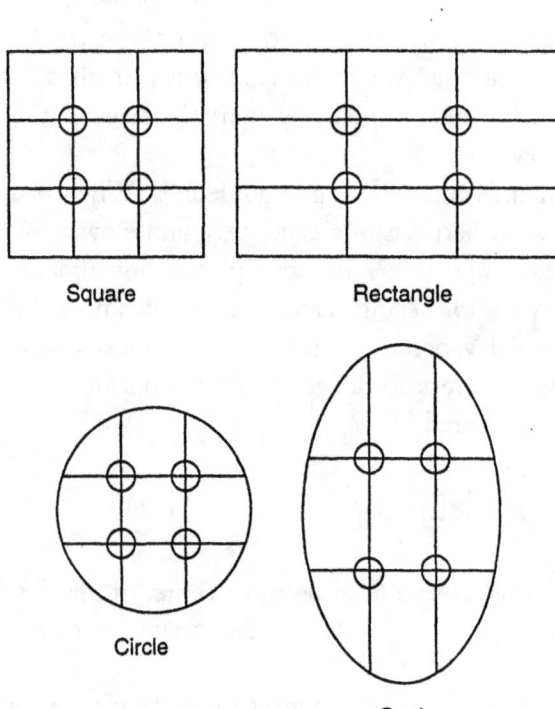

Square   Rectangle

Circle

Figure 5-2
Dividing the "Rule of Thirds"

Oval

The Rule of Thirds is theory, merely a beginning point for future departure and is kept in perspective, because in reality you don't conform to all the composition rules. Today, disregarding the rules is easy. More discipline is needed to adhere to the traditional guidelines and realize the good results.

A sensible approach to making a portrait is to determine the composition first because the compositional elements designate the format. When choosing the format, scale the portrait image to the format because the size and amount of the subject relates to the position of the subject.

The outside boundary of the format can be a frame which can extend above, below, or even with the surface plane of the portrait and is considered part of the spatial illusions.

The square format is static, but the image within alleviates the monotony. The rectangular format, by its varying width and length, creates movement. Because the human body is vertical, the vertical rectangle is appropriate for portraiture.

The corners in the square and rectangle formats are actually invisible arrows, Figure 5-3. The line is subjective by being felt, or objective by its actual presence. Any line approaching a corner gains in importance.

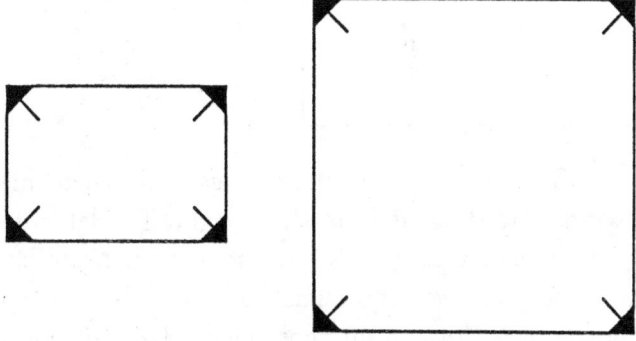

Figure 5-3
Corners of Rectangle and
Square

The circle and oval format are continuous movement in a clockwise or counterclockwise direction, Figure 5-4.

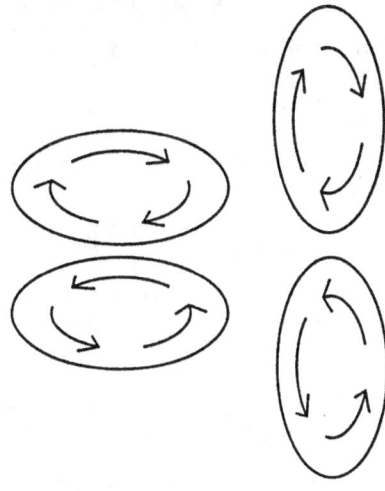

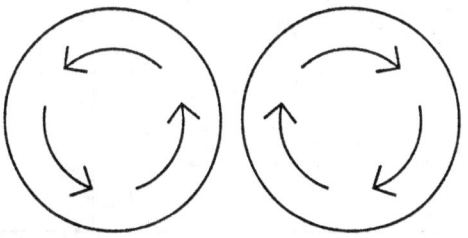

Figure 5-4
Movement Within Circle and
Oval

Placing the Subject

Within the format is the placement of the subject. Place the subject at any of the four horizontal and vertical intersections, Figure 5-5. Placing the subject off-center creates activity and the two unequal sections demonstrate movement.

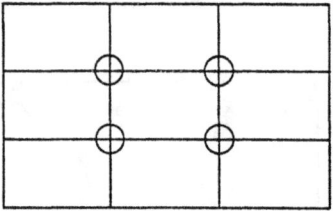

Figure 5-5
Placing the Subject

The format is divided vertically into left and right sides. Normal "reading" is from left to right. The left side shows faster motion, energy, action, ascent, and appears nearer and larger. The right side is slower, more static, and quiet because the viewer's eye moves more slowly from right to left. The right side attracts longer time for attention because the eye, moving quickly from left to right, lingers longer on the right side.

Place the subject in the upper half of the format to gain in importance, Figure 5-6. If the subject is placed in the lower half of the format, the subject loses in importance.

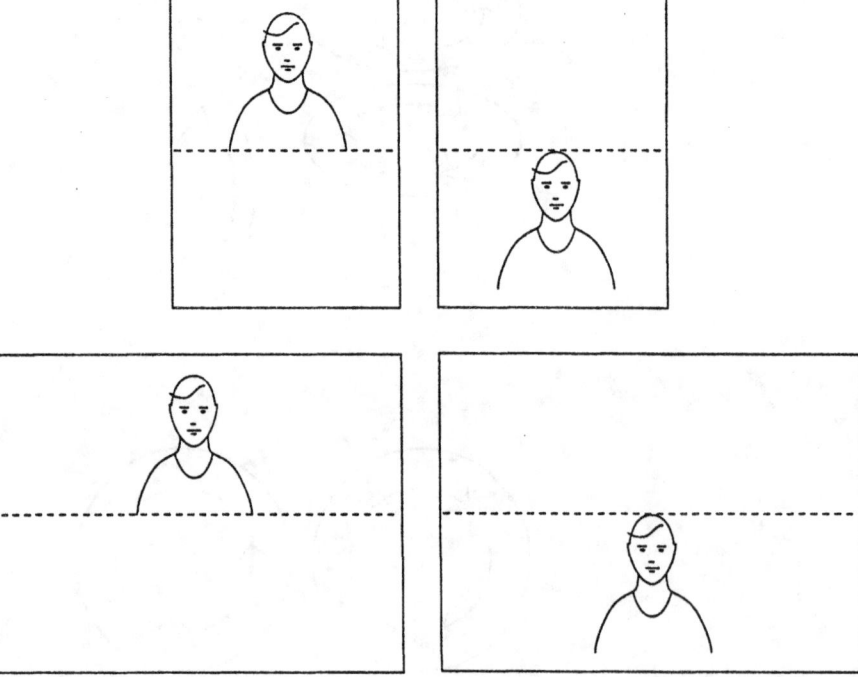

Figure 5-6
Placing the
Subject in Upper
Half of Format

The subject moves into the greater space section of the format, Figure 5-7. In a portrait of only one person, the person looks and "moves" in one direction, left or right. If the person is "centered" so that he is looking or moving to the left more space remains on the left side of the format than the right side. If the person is "centered" so that he is looking and moving to the right, more space remains on the right side of the format than the left side.

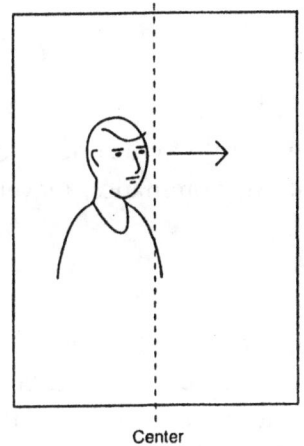 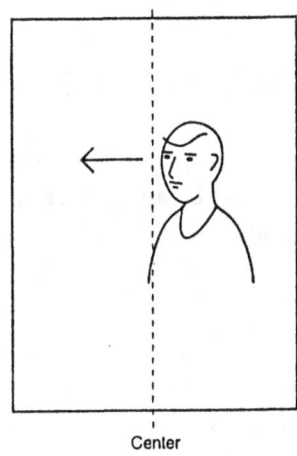

Figure 5-7
Subject Moves Into Greater
Space of Format

Avoid foreign elements that don't relate but can detract. An artist paints out unwanted objects or lines of design but you can't "paint" them out. You only have the option of moving the camera angle for the best composition.

Equal "weight" in the format is suggested visually or numerically. Two subjects of equal weight are not placed on equal sides of the intersection points. This creates sameness and two focal points. The two focal points should support each other and not conflict. Balanced tension is created by the placement of one subject at unequal positions.

The subject of least importance is placed at a distance from the more important subject. This balances the more important subject, especially if the more important subject is placed near the center.

The center of interest is emphasized by placing the greatest amount of detail at the center of interest. Detail is controlled by a soft or sharp focus.

Isolated subjects appear heavier than grouped subjects. Grouped, stacked, or crowded subjects appear heavier if the overall shape is irregular as opposed to regular shaped, Figure 5-8.

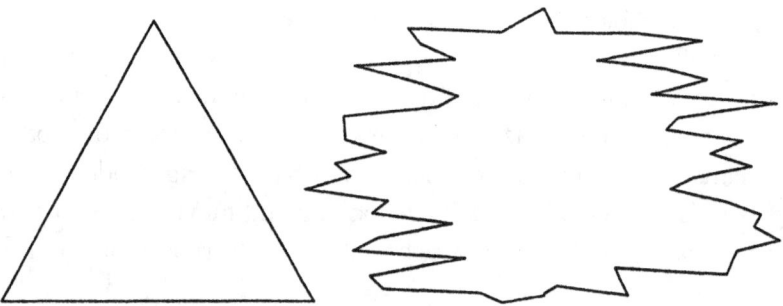

Figure 5-8
Regular or Irregular Shape of
Groups

Principles of Arrangement

The principles of arrangement add to the lines of design and involve balance, harmony, contrast, dominance, movement, and unity.

Balance

Balance is visual equality formed to achieve unity. Balance appeals to the viewer's sense of equilibrium. Equality is in the number, weight, importance, dominance, or value of the objects. Visual balance is also obtained by shape, lightness, darkness, texture, and color. If balance is the objective, then the lack of balance disturbs the viewer's eye unless it is intended.

Shape is symmetrical, asymmetrical, and radial. Symmetrical balance uses identical objects on either side of a central line to create stability, calmness, and formal shape to denote wholeness. In symmetrical, each half offers the reverse half of the other half.

Asymmetrical shape emerges when two halves of a portrait are created equally with forms, shapes, light, texture, and color. Asymmetry is non-uniform, active, dynamic, and informal.

A radial shape emerges when the elements originate from a central point and extend outward. A radial shape is an adaptation of a symmetrical shape.

Light and dark values balance each other. Visually, dark values are heavier than light values. A dark portrait expresses drama, somberness, and mystery. A light portrait expresses cheer, straightforwardness, and buoyancy.

Texture is the smooth or rough surface of an object. Side lighted objects emphasize texture. The rough texture appears heavier than the smooth texture and appears warmer, welcome, and crude. The smoother texture appears pristine and cool. A large expanse of smooth background is balanced by a small expanse of rough background. Conversely, a large expanse of rough background is balanced by a small expanse of smooth background.

Color is balanced mainly by advancing and receding colors. The advancing colors carry more visual weight than the receding colors. A small amount of an advancing color dominates a large amount of receding colors.

Harmony

Harmony unifies the elements in the portrait so they become related. The extremes of unity produce a portrait too unified and boring or a portrait too disjointed and chaotic. Unity should mingle with variety for the best composition.

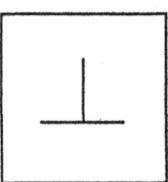

Figure 5-9
Opposite Lines

Harmony also occurs in opposition. For example, when two opposite lines, Figure 5-9, meet in severe harmony such as a vertical and horizontal line.

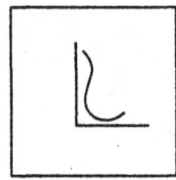

Figure 5-10
Transition Lines

Harmony moves in transition when the two opposing lines meet and a third compromising line combines to soften and unify, Figure 5-10.

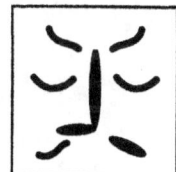

Figure 5-11
Major and Minor Lines

Harmony emerges by subordination to produce a major theme, then uses minor themes to contribute to the major theme, Figure 5-11.

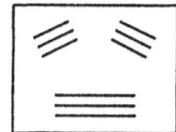

Figure 5-12
Repetition Lines

Harmony is further obtained by repetition, a process the opposite of subordination, Figure 5-12. Equal or unequal repetition gives rhythm to the order.

Harmony is created by the shape, whether it's symmetrical, asymmetrical, or radial, Figure 5-13.

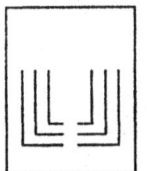
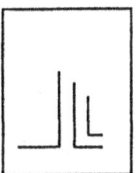
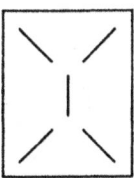

Figure 5-13
Symmetrical, Asymmetrical
and Radial Lines

Contrast

Emphasis is obtained with contrast. Variety in the shape, lightness, darkness, texture, and color achieve emphasis. Variety leads the viewer's eye away from conventional composing. When too much or too little variety exists no point is emphasized.

Dominance

Dominance is the major element of expression, regardless of the content, and ranks first in importance while the other elements rank second. The viewer's eye rests longest on the most important element and travels accordingly to the minor elements. The travel time of the viewer's eye is accomplished by contrast, size, value, shape, and location. The minor elements, also important, provide the standard for which the dominant element is contrasted or compared.

Movement

Movement is the direction that the viewer's eye travels to bind the parts into a rhythmic sequence. The elements of the portrait don't move, only the viewer's eye moves to unexpected points. The greater the contrast of the elements in a portrait, the greater the eye movement.

Movement is subtly suggested by fabric pulling from the body or pushing on the body, muscles pushing against the skin, and lighting on the subject.

Unity

Unity relates to order and results from combining the portrait elements to create the total effect. The whole of the portrait is more important than any one element. The most pleasing ratio of variety is employed to unify.

In a portrait that includes two individuals, there are two basic lines of design. But the separate subjects work together by bringing the separate compositional lines together. The integrated rhythm of the two persons in their common foreground and background unifies a portrait.

YOUR PARTICIPATION

Defining a Classic Outdoor Color Portrait

Your foundation building blocks for making a classic outdoor color portrait have been fully established by your knowledge of the concepts of portraiture, the implementation of your enriched ability to see and use your intellect, perception, intuition, observation, imagination, anticipation, and expression. You combined these elements with the creative process, lines of design, and composition. Now, you are ready to incorporate those building blocks using lighting, foreground, and background.

A classic outdoor color portrait means photographing persons in outdoor settings using universal artistic guidelines for your style. Such a portrait withstands the test of time. Every era, nation, and culture has its avant-garde portraitists to uproot the accepted style, but classic portraits never go out of style. They are constantly rediscovered.

Lighting

Light is the absence of darkness. With light, the world is seen. To see light is to use sight as a language of communication. Lighting acts as the primary building block of a classic outdoor color portrait.

Lighting gives life to the portrait by creating shadows that separate detail. The ambient lighting creates a third dimension by shaping and contouring the essential parts of the portrait to give each part its own plane.

Lighting is always moving and conveys information from one plane to another. Because people are accustomed to viewing each other in an outdoor environment with one prime source of lighting, the sun, the objective is to use the sun properly as the main source of lighting.

Lighting in portraiture is "general" in the way light falls, but not all areas and details are equal in quality lighting. Lighting becomes "specific" in areas with clear details because the light molds form. The type, amount, and quality of lighting placed on the subject, foreground, and background provides the mood for the portrait.

Lighting Ratio

The "Lighting Ratio" is a numerical equation of the relationship between the highlight side of the subject's face and the shadow side of the subject's face. The highlight side is the section of the subject most directly hit by the lighting source. The shadow side is the section of the subject with the rays of the lighting source cut off. The selection of the ratio to use depends on the mood of the portrait that you desire.

In portraiture the lighting situations on a face create different amounts of lighting on each side of the face. One side is darker than the other side and is expressed numerically in the lighting ratio. In addition to the lighting ratio of both sides of the face there is a lighting ratio of the planes on the front of the face, at the tip of the nose, and at the back of the face by the ears.

The lighting ratio defines the difference between the maximum and minimum amount of lighting on the face and is created by the lighting and its contrasting shadow. The lighting ratio creates dimension as the light side advances and the dark side recedes.

The side of the face that is shaded has the least amount of light on it, or is the darkest side represented as a numerical "1."

The side of the face that is illuminated has the most amount of light on it, or is the lightest side represented as a numerical "4."

1:4 — Considered the best lighting

1:3 — Considered acceptable lighting

1:2 — Not considered acceptable lighting

1:1 — Not considered acceptable lighting

Simply stated, the lighting ratio of 1:4 means that the light side or the reading of 4 is four times as light as the dark side reading of 1; the 1:3 ratio means the light side reading of 3 is three times as light as the dark side reading of 1; the 1:2 ratio means the light side reading of 2 is twice as light as the dark side reading of 1. A 1:1 ratio indicates equal lighting on each side.

Once you have determined the lighting ratio, the choice is yours to increase or decrease the ratio to achieve the effect you desire. Contrast control is recommended because satisfactory rendition of the lightest and darkest colors is difficult.

The control of lighting in outdoor portraiture is limited and often you have to do the best you can with the existing lighting conditions.

Two Types of Lighting

The "art of lighting" requires the study of the two types of lighting: natural and artificial.

Natural lighting is created by ambient lighting. Artificial lighting is created by the portraitist. The only lighting angle that should ever be placed on the face and body is the angle that flatters.

Natural Lighting

Natural lighting was the first lighting used in photography. The early daguerreotypist used natural lighting and the subject had to endure long, motionless posing sessions. This accounts, in part, for the serious expressions. Today, fast film for natural lighting allows you to expose the film in fractions of seconds and the subject experiences only short posing sessions.

The world is lit by one natural light source—the illumination from the sun—to add shapes, contours, shadows, and highlights to create three dimensions.

Natural lighting for portraiture is redirected lighting, and becomes the main source of lighting.

Natural lighting is available any time of the day. The sun when not covered by clouds, produces direct and bright lighting. If the sun moves behind the clouds, lighting is still available as filtered, flat lighting.

Because the sun has a constant, predictable rotation, you locate natural lighting and control the lighting by moving the subject, not the lighting.

Natural lighting is used as the basis of front, back, and side lighting. Natural lighting is quite flattering, especially when diffused.

In essence, natural outdoor lighting acts like a large studio room in which all planes of the subject become lighted from overlapping angles of light.

To always control the primary source of natural lighting, the sun, you arrange the building blocks with two types of natural lighting: subtractive lighting and additive lighting.

Subtractive Lighting

Subtractive lighting takes light away from the ambient lighting. Light is blocked from one direction to make the existing light emerge from all other directions.

In a suitable outdoor location, nature's natural light blockers such as foliage and trees are ideal. In a less desirable area with no blockers, you can block lighting and create a system to subtract lighting. Light is subtracted from the subject by two methods:

• To block light, place a Larson Enterprise, Inc. Reflectasol Black Square or large piece of black opaque cardboard or the equivalent, on the side away from the light source and parallel to the face. This blocking material can be held by an assistant or mounted on a stand. Keep the material close to the subject's face but at a comfortable distance for the subject, Figure 6-1.

• To block light, place a Larson Enterprises, Inc. Reflectasol Black Square or large piece of black, opaque cardboard or the equivalent, parallel to the ground and about two feet above the subject's head. This blocking material can be held by an assistant or mounted on a stand. The rear edge of the blocking material is placed directly over the back of the subject's head to make the main lighting source come from a lower angle, Figure 6-1.

A disadvantage of subtractive lighting is the loss of highlighting on the head and hair, unless the black material on the top of the head is brought forward enough to allow highlights on the back of the head and hair.

In subtractive lighting, the low lighting level necessitates a slower shutter speed with less depth of field which is the area in sharp focus from the foreground to background. This is a problem if a fast shutter speed is needed.

Additive Lighting

Additive lighting adds light to the ambient lighting. To achieve additive lighting, you enhance the subject by increasing the lighting.

In natural outdoor locations the purpose of additive lighting is to use the advantages of open shade and then add reflected light to correct and supplement the limited natural lighting.

Additive lighting is accomplished by two methods:

• Use a Larson Enterprises, Inc. Reflectasol silver, white, or gold square; or a large piece of white, opaque cardboard; or a large piece of cardboard covered with crumpled aluminum foil or equivalent. This additive lighting material can be held by an

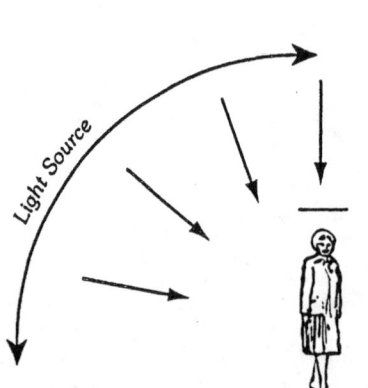

Figure 6-1
Subtractive Lighting

assistant or mounted on a stand. Additive lighting is made by reflecting sunlight from head or camera height to counteract the top light by filling in the shadows under the eyes, nose, and chin, Figure 6-2.

• Use a Larson Enterprises, Inc. Reflectasol silver, white, or gold square; or a large piece of white, opaque cardboard; or a large piece of cardboard covered with crumpled aluminum foil or equivalent. This additive lighting material can be held by an assistant or mounted on a stand. Use the sunlight redirected into the shaded area of your location from an angle higher than your subject's head, Figure 6-2.

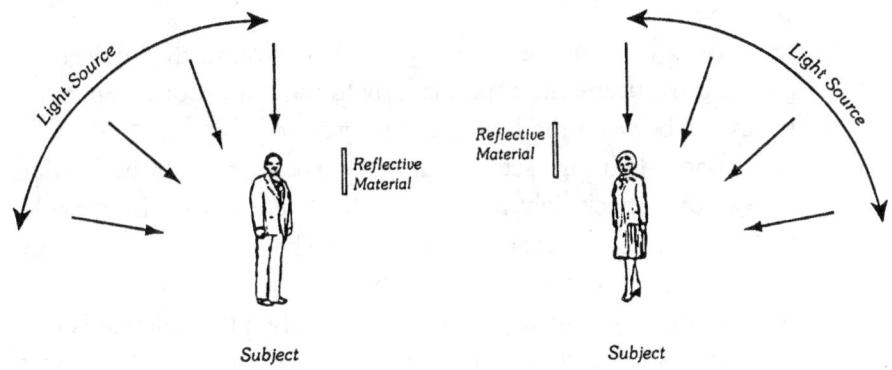

Figure 6-2
Additive Lighting

The use of light on the face and back lighting offers an additional advantage of raising the entire light level.

Additive light is a disadvantage when the required reflective material is too near the subject.

If the reflected lighting is too strong for the lighting level of the location, a distracting artificial lighting look is produced.

Characteristics of Natural Light

Natural light is defined further by the direction of the lighting source which includes: front lighting, back lighting, and side lighting.

Front Lighting

Front lighting originates in front of the subject. Front lighting flattens the subject into the background because the shadows aren't pronounced enough to give the subject a rounded appearance and this reduces the subject to a two-dimensional figure. Front lighting on the face makes facial lines less visible because shadows are eliminated. The subject squints his eyes with the lighting source directly into his eyes. Colors are brightened and detail emphasized with front lighting. Front lighting simplifies a complex, patterned subject.

Back Lighting

In back lighting the lighting source originates directly behind the subject or behind the subject slightly to one side.

Direct back lighting gives prominence to the subject by silhouetting. The entire subject rimmed with light adds importance, especially if the subject appears small in the outdoor setting. The subject does not squint his eyes in back lighted situations.

Back lighting creates a halo of light around the subject and gives a translucent effect, particularly to the hair. Some separation is desired between the hair and background.

Back lighting sets a dark subject apart from a dark background. Back lighting reduces the intensity of a bright color because the color becomes part of the shade. The back lighting situation creates contrast between the subject and background. The contrast in back lighted portraits is diminished if a reflector is used to bounce some of the back lighting onto the front of the subject.

The proper exposure reading is made by reading the light level on the front of the subject rather than reading the light level of the entire composition.

When back lighting hits the lens directly, a glare is created which is called a flare. Alleviate flare problems by placing the lighting source behind an object such as a tree. Or use a lens shade to shield the lens from flare. You can use your hand to shield the lens. In general, keep the lighting source out of the format.

Side Lighting

In side lighting the lighting source originates at the side of the subject when the camera is in a north to south position, Figure 6-3.

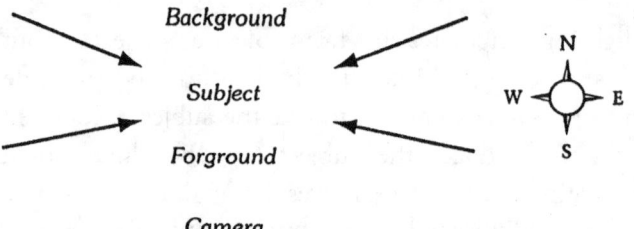

Figure 6-3
Side Lighting

The preferable side lighting on the subject comes from an approximate angle of 0 degrees to 60 degrees depending on the angle of the face, Figure 6-4. These recommended angles avoid side lighting developing into back lighting or front lighting.

The best side lighting occurs at midmorning and mid-afternoon.

If reflectors are used to fill in light, be sure the strongest lighted side is the same side as the lighting source.

Of the three directions of lighting—front, back, and side—side lighting is a first preference because the shadows give depth, volume, and form to the subject.

Additional refinements of the lighting source: direction of the lighting source, shadow, time of day, direct lighting, flat lighting, and seasons.

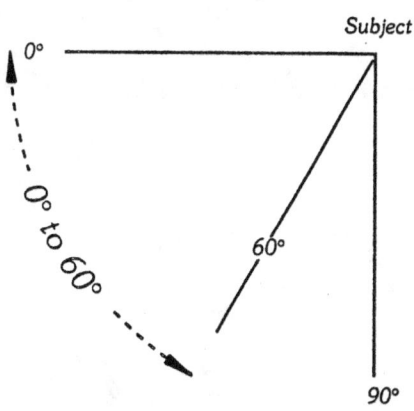

Figure 6-4
Lighting Angle

Direction of the Lighting Source

The lighting source is direct, reflected, or filtered from the front, back, or side and is intense or softened. The angle the light hits the subject affects the features by emphasizing or softening features.

The source of its direction affects the quality of lighting such as from the north, cold; from the east, harsh; from the south and west, warm and bright.

Shadow

A shadow is the dark area or dark shape cast upon another surface by an object displacing light from the dark area or shape.

In a portrait it's important to study what occupies the space in front, back, and side of the subject because the subject and objects inside and outside the portrait format cast shadows.

There is no shadow when lighting comes equally from all angles.

The sunlight affects the color of the object, the shadow cast, and the color of the highlight.

The shadow makes a different shape if thrown onto a flat surface or a wavy surface.

Only Western artists recognize light and shadow as the best accomplishment. Certainly not everyone sees as Westerners.

Time of Day

Any degree of lighting at any time of the day emits color

which affects our emotions. The color of the atmosphere is altered by the distance the sun's rays travel to the earth and the time of day. When at the farthest distance, the sun's rays travel through more atmosphere to scatter the rays. At noon, the sun's rays range closer to the earth than at sunrise or sunset.

The lighting from the east intensifies a color; from the south or west, reddens the color; and from the north, the lighting has the most neutral effect.

The colors of the sky from which the lighting is reflected influences the color of the atmosphere. A gray sky reflects gray light, a sky of white clouds reflects white, and a clear blue sky reflects blue. The lighting variations are exciting/depressing, warm/cold, and bright/dull.

Predawn lighting has a similar effect to flat lighting. The third dimension narrows to a minimum because the volume is missing. Predawn offers a simpler form of lighting because only two planes exist in flat lighting. Predawn lighting appears cool, melancholy, gray, and cheerless.

Dawn light simplifies, molds, and shapes. It's a quiet, mysterious, and cool light. A few minutes before and after dawn, the form and texture disappear from back lighted subjects to become outline silhouettes.

The sunrise or early morning light is the two hours after sunrise. This lighting casts a yellow, orange hue when the atmosphere is clean and moist. These two hours appear pure, cheerful, and alert.

Midmorning light emits a yellowish cast because the atmosphere is still clean and contains moisture. Side lighting and high contrast in shadows are the result of midmorning light. All color values are lightened. Midmorning lighting is excellent portrait lighting.

The midday sun sits directly overhead and perpendicular to the earth. Noon lighting is white lighting two hours before or after noon. Midday lighting radiates the harshest, brightest rays from the sun. This "down lighting" known as an "aging light" creates shadows under the eyes and nose. Lighting between noon and midafternoon creates hot spots that appear yellow.

Midafternoon lighting, depending on the season, arrives approximately from 3:00 P.M. to 5:00 P.M. and casts red lighting. Good side lighting at midafternoon produces good, long shadows, and is excellent portrait lighting.

Sunset is the two hours before the sun goes down and creates red and rosy-orange colors. The colors appear drier than the morning colors. The atmosphere appears quiet, peaceful, inactive, nostalgic, and warm. The sunset gives off middle values, medium shadow contrasts, and long shadows. A few minutes before and after sunset, form and texture disappear from back lighted subjects to become outline silhouettes.

Dusk is the dim light before dark. Dusk is a quiet and cool light. At dusk, in addition to dawn, distinguishing one color from another is difficult because the lighting source is weak.

Direct Lighting

Direct lighting is when the sun's rays fall unfiltered on the subject. It creates powerful and deep shadows with sharp edges. Direct lighting has high, strong shadow contrasts with light color values. Direct sun lighting is less harsh if originating from the back, side, or at a slight angle to the subject.

Direct lighting flattens the subject's features because texture and detail are lost.

Flat Lighting

Flat lighting occurs when the sun's rays fall on the subject through a filter such as clouds, haze, smoke, dust, rain, mist, or snow. Flat lighting diffuses the light by scattering the light rays, and the direction of the lighting source remains in question. A cloudy day appears soft blue, mysterious, and romantic.

Flat lighting creates a softer shadow, which is pale and vague with ill-defined, feathery edges. The contrast between the lighting and shadow is minimum, and the lighting provides medium contrast shadow and medium color value. With no shadow, everything is seen in greater detail because nothing is withheld, and the contrast between light and dark seems less abrupt. The subtle shading gives form to the face and body without sharpening the details. The skin has a soft-focus edge without every blemish showing.

With flat lighting the subject can be moved easily on location because there is no direct sun lighting source. The subject doesn't have any reason to squint his eyes.

Seasons

The seasons—spring, summer, autumn, and winter—determine the hour of the day to photograph, because each season has its own lighting and psychology. Summer and winter are the extremes with spring and autumn being transitional. The best portrait season ranges from March-April through October-November, depending on the locale.

The season is influenced by the distance the sun soars from the earth, and how low or high the sun's arc is from the earth, Figure 6-5. The height of the sun from the horizon determines brightness, color temperature, texture, and contrast. The height of the sun depends on the time of day, season, and geographical location.

Spring has a rebirth quality because the vegetation is the new, green color, and flowers bloom everywhere.

Summer is the maximum extreme of lighting and has steadiness, durability, and clarity. The summer sun stays closer to the earth, the angle of the sun is closer to the earth, and the sun stays longer overhead at a high arc. The longer overhead sun's arc is avoided because it casts shadows under the eyes and nose. June has the most hours of daylight and the changes in light are slower than in the short days of December.

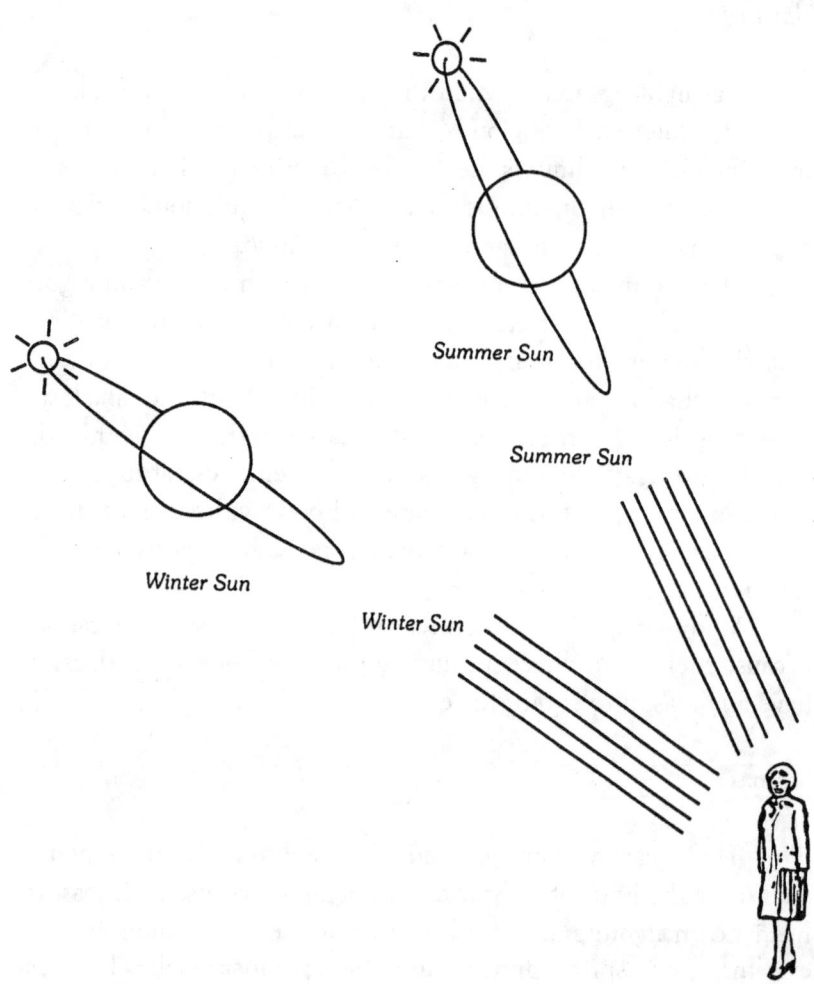

Summer Sun

Summer Sun

Winter Sun

Winter Sun

Figure 6-5
Arc of the Sun

Autumn, with its changing earth colors from green to red/ yellow, provides subdued lighting.

Winter lighting is flat because the lighting source is furthest from the subject, at a low angle, and never soars overhead. In winter a portrait can be made closer to noon than in the summer. December has the fewest hours of daylight and the changes in light are quicker than in the long days of June. Less light makes a shorter day demanding that a portrait can be made later in the morning and earlier in the afternoon.

Special consideration for clothes and the length of the posing session should be made for extreme temperatures.

In general, good natural lighting in any season should fall on the subject's face in a pleasing manner and wrap around the torso, arms, hands, legs, and feet.

Artificial Lighting

Man created the original artificial lighting with fire. Artificial lighting advanced from fire to oil lamps, candles, gas lamps, electric lamps, and then fluorescent lamps.

Artificial lighting, which simulates natural lighting for photographic portraiture, came into prominence with the tungsten light bulb invented in 1879, the flash bulb, and electronic strobe.

The quick burst of an electronic strobe light offers the best imitation of natural daylight, and is accomplished from a compact operating unit. The electronic strobe unit operates so strongly and quickly that a subject's expression can be captured before any shock responses occur such as blinking eyes.

Artificial lighting is used as fill lighting when photographing back lighted persons. Without fill lighting, the person appears in silhouette.

Artificial lighting can be used with natural lighting to add a subtle sparkle of light.

The electronic strobe has a disadvantage in outdoor lighting if front-mounted because it's hard to control as the light hits the subject frontally, and flattens the subject into two dimensions. The electronic strobe, if too powerful, washes out natural lighting and soft shadows to create a hard, well-defined shadow behind the subject.

The electronic strobe, when mounted on the front of the camera and held at the subject's level, causes "red eye," which is when light from the electronic strobe enter's the subject's eyes and is reflected back into the camera lens. The final print shows a red dot in the subject's eyes. This is avoided by having the subject look away from the camera or by placing the electronic strobe away from the camera and at an angle to the subject.

There are several ways to use an electronic strobe:

• Place the electronic strobe more above and to one side of the camera, bounce the light off the walls if the walls are white or of a usable, neutral color.

• Bounce the electronic strobe light off the ceiling if the ceiling is no more than twelve feet high and is white or of a usable, neutral color.

• Use a diffusing element, such as a piece of masking tape or cloth over the flash part of the electronic strobe.

Studio Lighting

The studio is no more than a dark room with lighting added. Artificial lighting used in a studio is derived from using a combination of major floodlights, that spread a wide beam, and minor spotlights, that pinpoint a narrow beam.

Studio lighting is easier to control than outdoor lighting because the lights can be moved to various positions.

The floodlights and spotlights of studio lighting create general types of lighting and is best when highlights are placed on the five frontal planes of the face—forehead, nose, chin, and both cheeks. The neck and sides usually remain in some shadow. This follows the general concept that highlights advance and shadowed areas recede.

Types of Studio Lighting

To obtain as much control as possible of the unadjustable omnidirectional lighting source of the sun, it's important to know the basic types of studio lighting used on the subject's face: Broad, Short, Butterfly, Rembrandt, and Split.

For explanation purposes only, a single main light is used in Figures 6-6, 6-7, 6-8, 6-9, and 6-10 to show the pure forms of Broad, Short, Butterfly, Rembrandt, and Split Lighting. In actual usage a combination of main and fill lights is used.

The main light's position is varied in its light-to-the-subject distance, height, and angle to the subject. The light position varies slightly for men, women, and children.

Broad Lighting

If the face is turned slightly from the camera or at a partial view, one side shows more than the other and this side that shows more is called the broad side. If the main light source is placed on the broad side of the face the lighting is called broad lighting.

In Figure 6-6, the main light source is placed about two feet above eye level and hits fully the broad side of the face facing the camera. Broad lighting is advantageous to widen a narrow or thin face. Figure 6-6.

Short Lighting

If the face is turned slightly from the camera or at a partial view, one side shows less than the other and this side that shows the least is called the short side. If the main light source is placed on the short side of the face the lighting is called short lighting.

In Figure 6-7, the main light source fully hits the short side of the face away from the camera and is placed about two feet above eye level. This is considered excellent lighting for portraiture because most people are flattered by short lighting as a means to narrow a broad face. Figure 6-7.

Butterfly Lighting

In Figure 6-8, the main light source hits the front of the face. The light source is placed higher than two feet above the subject's eye level to create a butterfly-shape shadow directly underneath the nose as both sides of the face are illuminated. The butterfly-shape shadow does not extend into the lipline. Figure 6-8.

Rembrandt Lighting

Rembrandt lighting is a combination of short and butterfly lighting. In Figure 6-9, the main light source is placed higher than two feet above the subject and to one side of the face at an angle. The closest side of the face to the camera is lit, and a triangular shape of light falls across the nose on the cheek of the furthest side. Figure 6-9.

Split Lighting

In Figure 6-10, the main light source is placed with only one half of the face lighted vertically. The light source is placed at eye level, 90 degrees from the nose angle. Split lighting should not be used on subjects with deep-set eyes, heavy cheeks, or hair that falls in front of the face. Figure 6-10.

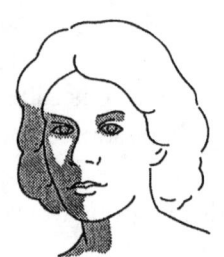

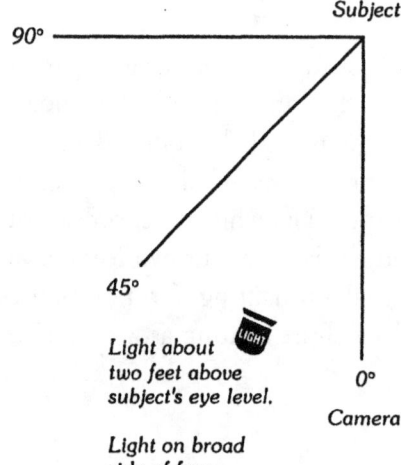

90° ———————————— Subject

45°

Light about
two feet above
subject's eye level.

0°

Camera

Light on broad
side of face.

Figure 6-6
Broad Lighting

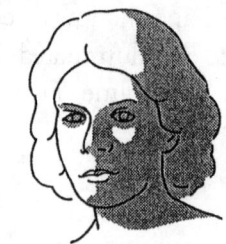

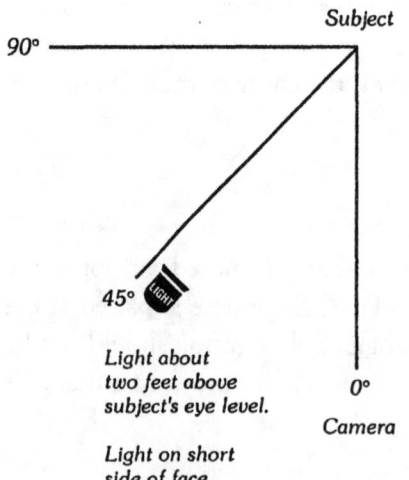

90° ———————————— Subject

45°

Light about
two feet above
subject's eye level.

0°

Camera

Light on short
side of face.

Figure 6-7
Short Lighting

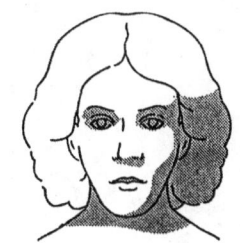

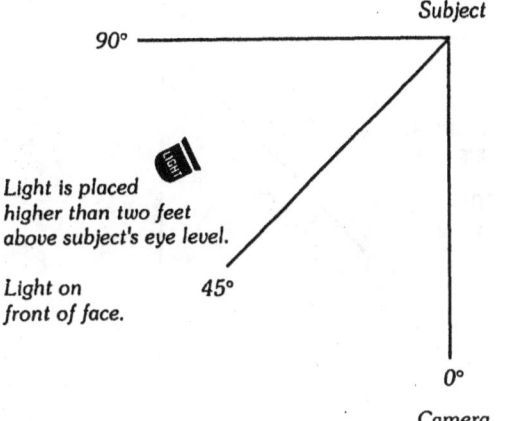

Subject

90°

*Light is placed
higher than two feet
above subject's eye level.*

*Light on
front of face.*

45°

0°

Camera

Figure 6-8
Butterfly Lighting

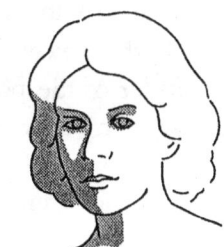

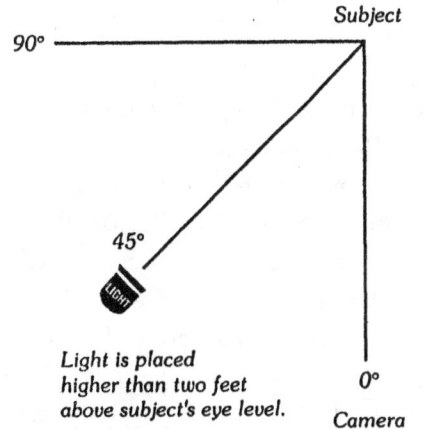

Subject

90°

45°

*Light is placed
higher than two feet
above subject's eye level.*

0°

Camera

*Light is placed
on closest side
of face at an angle.*

Figure 6-9
Rembrandt Lighting

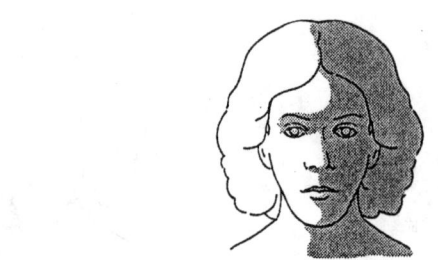

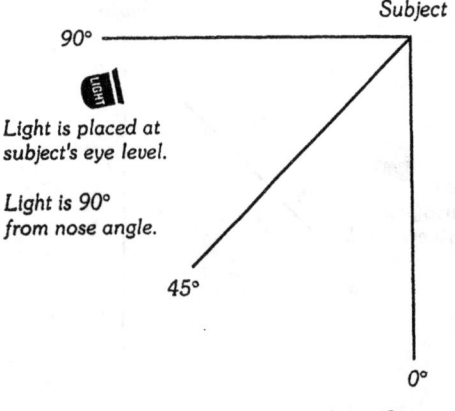

Subject

90°

*Light is placed at
subject's eye level.*

*Light is 90°
from nose angle.*

45°

0°

Camera

Figure 6-10
Split Lighting

Foreground

The foreground is the portrait area closest or what appears the closest to the viewer. The purpose of the foreground is to provide the viewer's eye with a beginning reference point for the remainder of the portrait. Foreground adds depth to the portrait similar to the depth added by background and lighting.

The wooden, metal, or plastic frame around the portrait serves as the foremost foreground plane. A white or light colored frame broadens the portrait and the viewer's eye follows outward. A black or dark colored frame shrinks the portrait and the viewer's eye follows inward. If the frame angles inward the viewer's eye follows inward. If the frame angles outward the viewer's eye follows outward, Figure 6-11.

The positioning of the foreground objects alters the illusion of three dimensions as the foreground creates receding planes to the background. To place a single object in the center of the foreground produces an illusion that the object moves forward from the background. Objects placed near the edge create the illusion that the center recedes.

Use a minimal amount of texture in a foreground because it will compete with the main subject. If textured objects are used in the foreground, avoid positioning textured items against other textured items.

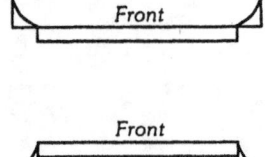

Figure 6-11
Frame Around Portrait

Position the foreground masses so they don't appear unsupported.

If possible, leave space between the foreground and the subject to further the illusion of three dimensions.

A foreground works best when out of focus. Using a "selective focus" at the widest possible aperture throws the foreground out of focus. The wash of a soft focus foreground frames the subject and isolates the sharply focused subject.

In location portraiture, there are no filters to eliminate unwanted objects so the soft focus foreground offers an excellent way to eliminate a problem area. Foreground framing with limbs, shrubs, or believable objects conceals unwanted situations and enhances composition elements such as stooped shoulders, large hips, bare knees, and arthritic hands.

Another important aspect of the foreground is vignetting which is a gradual darkening of the outer edges and corners of the portrait. These selected areas are made out-of-focus to concentrate the viewer's eye on the subject. The out-of-focus, darkened area fades into the portrait with no distinct border.

Vignetting eliminates detailed clutter and adds to the total portrait by emphasizing the subject as the viewer's eye moves from the darker to lighter area.

Vignetting is accomplished by professional mechanical devices such as the Leon Vignetter, homemade devices, natural elements such as greenery, or in the darkroom.

Regardless of how it's accomplished, vignetting is best when subtle and not noticed because you don't view a person with darkened corners around him.

Background

The background is the area furthest from the viewer or that which appears furthest from the viewer. The area considered as background covers the entire area behind the subject and extends forward around part or all of the subject's sides. The background acts as a frame for the subject and is the support and foundation for the portrait, but should not dominate.

The background is a prominent element in establishing the character of the subject because the background sets an emotional mood with its lines of design and becomes an extension of the subject. The background should be authentic and comfortable for the subject. For example, a woman looks more comfortable in a background with a feminine S curve and a man appears at ease in a background of straight lines.

Once you establish that the subject can be photographed in an outdoor setting, ask yourself, "Am I making a photograph of the person or the landscape?" There is a tendency to include more background than necessary and turn the portrait into a pictorial portrait. A large expanse of background is unnecessary. With less background, the subject moves forward.

The supportive background doesn't dominate unless intended and is neutral as if holding the subject. The background is soft and vague with no sharply focused lines of design. The background compliments and is carefully considered because rarely is background a coincidence.

Portraits are easily made outdoors because of the variety of the backgrounds. Trees, bushes, and plants offer a limitless variety of green background. Green is a neutral background color available in most locations, although other colors are appropriate. Only the color of the subject's clothes limits the color of the background.

The background and the surroundings alter the color of the subject such as all green foliage casts green, a red brick wall casts red, and the morning and evening sun cast yellow and red respectively.

In placing the subject in the background, place the subject a distance of at least eight feet from the plane of the background. Subjects placed flat or close to the background, whether it's a wall or hedge, appear weak.

There are no guidelines, such as dark background for adults and light background for children.

In portraits, the subject in light-colored clothing projects, while the subject in dark-colored clothing recedes. But in the background, the opposite proves true. In backgrounds, light recedes, dark projects. As a general guideline, make the area around the subject lighter than the edges of the background, Figure 6-12.

Figure 6-12
Light and Dark in Background

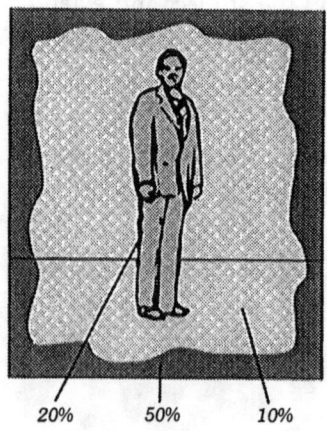

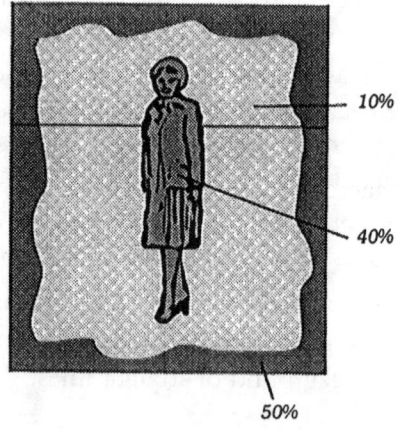

20%   50%   10%

10%

40%

50%

The light center area gives dimension and character. The dark edges give closeness and guides the viewer's eye to the center where the light or dark clothed subject is located. Frame the subject as if looking through a black tube and seeing the light at the end of the tube, or as if looking through a black, empty cardboard slide mount format. This light center and dark edges allow a differentiation between subject and background.

Lighting affects the green background. If back lighted, the green appears more luminous, transparent, and lighter. If front lighted, the dominant green appears darker. Moisture on the green reflects lighter. Relieve the intensity of the overall green background with a color that relates to the subject's clothes color such as a red dress accented with a small red flower in the background or a man's tan suit complimented by a tan fence post.

The background props, if any, are governed by the style of clothing worn by the subject and the intended mood. Formal attire requires a more formal background, while casual attire dictates a casual background. Props such as fences, gates, and statues are effective if they don't dominate.

The horizon line in a classic outdoor color portrait is avoided or used as an additional line of design. In the background, if the horizon line is at the middle two static equal halves are created. The viewer's eye has to determine which half is more important and the viewer's eye quickly loses interest. If the horizon line is high, the foreground is emphasized, and the foreground's content moves closer to the viewer. If the horizon line is unavoidable, a good location for the horizon line is according to the Rule of Thirds, about one third from the top or bottom, depending on what is emphasized. Placing the horizon line in the top or bottom 2/3 indicates which area is the most important. Greater value is placed on the 2/3 or wider area, Figure 6-13.

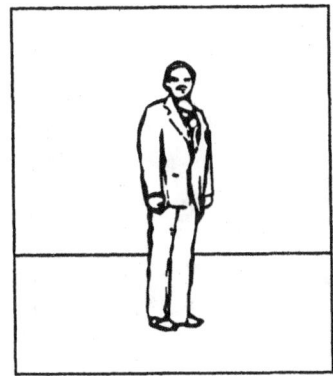 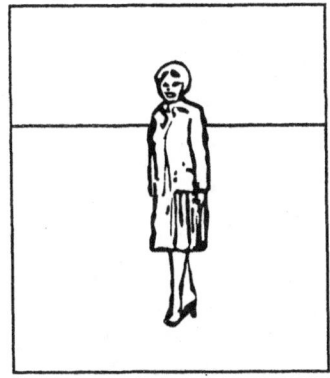

Figure 6-13
Horizon Line

If the background seems too spotty, check for the spots by looking through the camera viewfinder with the lens out of focus. Eliminate the spotty background by asking the subject to move or move the camera slightly for a different background.

Observe all the lines which radiate from the person that look like an extension of the body such as a pole extending from the top of the head or shoulder.

Here's a good general guideline for background problems. If there is an irritation, such as one white spot that can't be eliminated in an all dark background, then counter the white spot with another irritation, such as an additional one or two white spots. This way the white spots don't look like mistakes.

THE SUBJECT

Defining the Subject

Your preparation for a portrait began with the building blocks of lighting, foreground, and background. Now you come to what I call the "middle ground," your subject. You will need to analyze your subject, determine the pose you feel will be most effective, and aid in selecting the subject's clothing.

The study of the subject shows that classic proportions have not changed and posing of the human figure has progressed from the ancient, rigid statues with clenched fists, arms straight at the sides in parallel planes, and expressionless faces to a more natural stance with a fluid, counterbalance and projected into space with one leg advancing forward, arms bent, and the axis of the body forming an S curve.

Analyzing the Subject

Your response to the middle ground is analyzing the lines of design in the subject as represented by the head, face, torso, arms, hands, legs, and feet existing in planes and position relationships. This architectural unit has its own separate expressive language for communication.

Anatomy of the Head

The anatomy of the head consists of the hair, forehead, eyes, nose, lips, ears, and muscles. To know the "normals" of the face, known as the standards, aids in examining the characteristics of your subject's face.

The head is basically an egg-shaped ellipse with variations of four forms: round, square, triangle, and narrow, Figure 7-1.

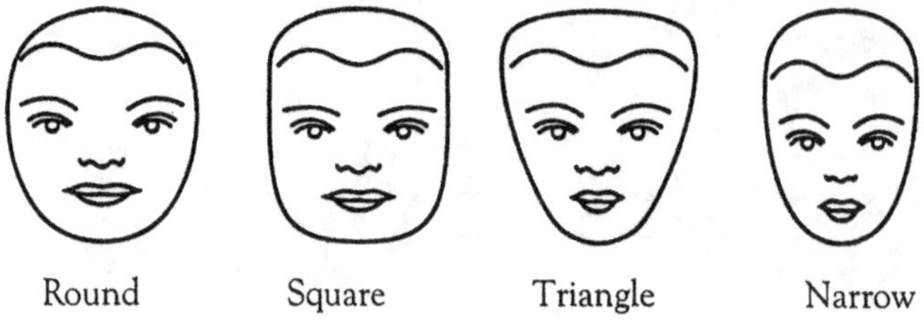

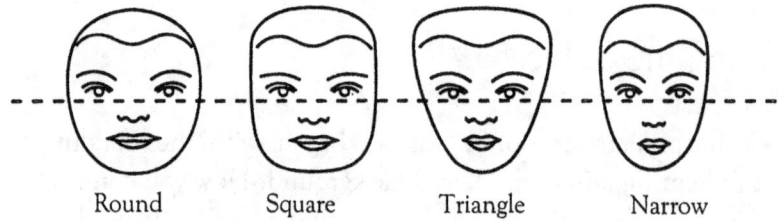

Figure 7-1
Head Shapes: Round, Square, Triangle, Narrow

Round   Square   Triangle   Narrow

If the normal head is divided into two equal halves, Figure 7-2, the division is beneath the eyes: one half extends from the bottom of the eyes to the top of the head; one half extends from the bottom of the eyes to the bottom of the chin.

Round   Square   Triangle   Narrow

Figure 7-2
Division of Head Into Equal Sections

The normal face section of the head is divided into three sections, Figure 7-3: hairline to eyebrows; eyebrows to the base of the nose; base of the nose to bottom of the chin.

In a well-proportioned head sections 1, 2, and 3 are basically equal in size. A variation example: a regular shaped face with unequal features such as a long nose alters the space and will increase section 2.

The head is dominated by the face which reveals character through outstanding lines of design.

The prominence of the forehead is mainly the angle of the head. If the subject's head tilts down the forehead looks bigger. If the subject's head tilts up the forehead looks smaller. The emphasis of a man's or woman's forehead is determined by the hairline. In a receding hairline, thin hairline, or bald head the forehead becomes more important and is subdued.

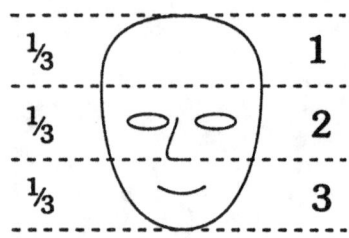

$\frac{1}{3}$ 1

$\frac{1}{3}$ 2

$\frac{1}{3}$ 3

Figure 7-3
Division of Face Into Three Sections

The eyes and eyelids give clues to any special characteristics of your subject. The eyelids roll up or down to cover or uncover the eye. When the eyelids are raised, one or more wrinkles form at the fold line. When the eyes and eyelids are wide open, the iris is more exposed causing the subject to appear alert, eager, and enthusiastic. When the eyes and eyelids are less open, the iris shows less causing the subject to appear shy and unenthusiastic.

The distance between the eyes is shorter when the head is turned at an angle.

The nose doesn't move to create expressions but acts to create light and shadow.

The lips show considerable emotion and are controlled by muscles surrounding the mouth like parentheses. There is a crease at the outer corners that is an up or down line. The lines of design of the two planes of the upper and lower lips reflect light and create shadows. A full frontal face view places the center of the mouth closer to the camera than the outer corners. A full smile showing teeth is marvelous in real life but in a portrait it's debatable if a full smile will "wear well" to the viewer over time.

The eyes and the mouth express the most emotion and should move voluntarily with each other.

The ears begin between the eyebrows and the bottom of the eyes. The ears have lines of design radiating to and from the head. The ear gains in importance as the head is turned from full frontal face view to full profile view. Ears protrude slightly to create shadows. Light coming from behind the ear makes part of the ear transparent.

The mind organizes its emotions to control the face muscles which are capable of an endless variety of expressions. When the subject smiles, the muscles of the face move upward toward the eyes covering the lower iris and horizontally elongates the entire eye.

In an older subject the muscles of the face have weakened to reveal more contours. The eyes become deeper set, the checks are more hollow, and the mouth is more prominent as the gumline shrinks. Additionally, body posture rounds, especially the shoulders.

Facial Views

The planes of the face—forehead, eyes, nose, mouth, cheek, temple, and chin—are the outer edge of the subject and are the only true likeness.

To study the planes of the face, observe the face from all angles in good lighting. The ideal situation is to place the subject facing you. At a comfortable distance from the subject, walk around the subject beginning at one side, crossing the front, and ending at the opposite side. In essence you have constructed a 180 degree arc around the subject.

However, to make your client more comfortable you should study the different head shapes early in your portrait evaluation so you can determine the subject's head shape at a quick glance without a lot of "on site" examination.

The starting view point for your observation is the subject's left side, followed by views until you end up at the subject's right side. For brevity, variations of the many points are defined by five basic facial views, Figure 7-4.

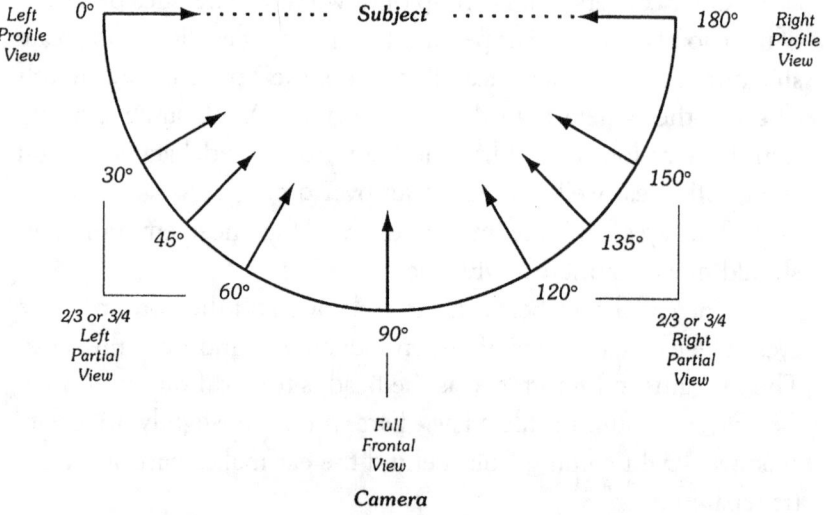

Figure 7-4
Facial Views

• At point 0 degree or at subject's left side called left profile.
• At points 30, 45, 60 degrees or roughly between left profile and full frontal view, called left 2/3 or 3/4 view or left partial view.
• At point 90 degree or at full frontal called full frontal view.
• At points 120, 135, 150 degrees or roughly between right profile and full frontal view, called right 2/3 or 3/4 or right partial view.
• At point 180 degrees or at subject's right side called right profile.

For simplification these angles are summarized into five views:
• Left profile view: 0 degree
• Left partial view: 30, 45, 60 degree
• Full frontal view: 90 degree
• Right partial view: 120, 135, 150 degree
• Right profile view: 180 degree

Each side of the face and each angle of the face is different.
• The full frontal face view at 90 degrees is seen with the face towards the camera with each half of the face equal.
• The left partial views of 30, 45, and 60 degrees and right partial views of 120, 135, and 150 degrees are seen with only one side of the face seen in its entirety.
• The left profile view of 0 degree and the right profile view of 180 degrees shows the face at a 90 degree angle to the camera. In the profile view, only one side of the face is seen.

To determine the best side, check both sides by looking at the subject from his left and right side. Observe the line of the far cheek. The side from which the cheek line protrudes the furthest into the background is the side of the subject's face that looks the heaviest.

Anatomy of the Torso, Arms, Hands, Legs, and Feet

A working knowledge of the standards for body measurements is advisable to quickly evaluate the lines of design of the subject's torso, arms, hands, legs, and feet, Figure 7-5.

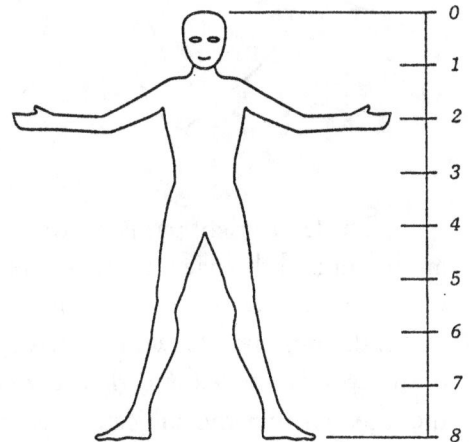

Figure 7-5
Body Measurements

Using the head as a measuring unit, the body, according to the Greek standards, stands eight heads in height. The masculine body measures two heads width across the shoulders with one and a half heads across the hips. The feminine body measures in width the opposite of the masculine measurement—one and a half heads across the shoulders and two head widths across the hips. All these measurements have variations. From these measurements you determine how to light and pose the torso, arms, hands, legs, and feet.

Selection of the Appropriate Facial View

The facial inspection with the torso, arms, hands, legs, and feet inspection enables you to select the best facial view with the best lighting, foreground, and background.

The full frontal face view showing equal sides of the face is highly acceptable, Figure 7-6. The full frontal face view shows more personality than the left and right partial views and profile view because the muscles show expressive movement on both sides of the face.

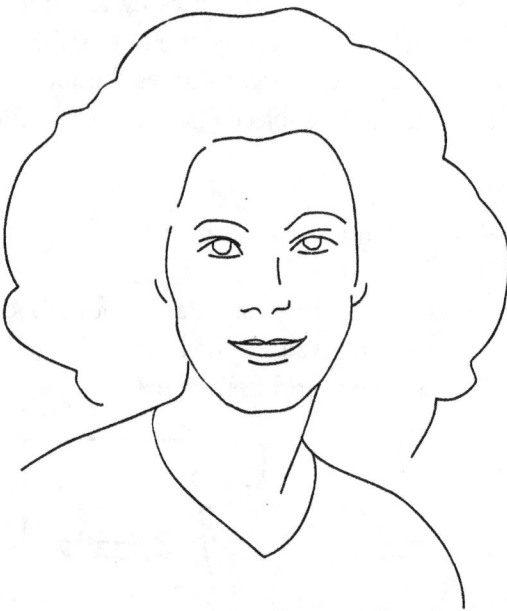

Figure 7-6
Full Frontal View

The left or right partial views are flattering because most faces are broad and this view narrows the face. The left or right partial view, Figure 7-7, has the eyes looking in the same direction in which the nose points, with the iris close to the center in the white of the eyes. In the left and right partial view, the leading interest is the face, whether the subject looks with the eyes at the camera or away from the camera. The direction of the eyes isn't as important as the expression in the eyes. The face isn't turned so far to the side that it loses the facial contour line. Don't let the white of the eye bleed out of the facial contour or let the nose protrude past the facial contour line. The nose is positioned more in the front side of the face than the back side of the face.

The profile is a view of half of the face and demonstrates more bony structure of the face. The left and right profile view, if possible, shows the tip of the far eyelash, Figure 7-8.

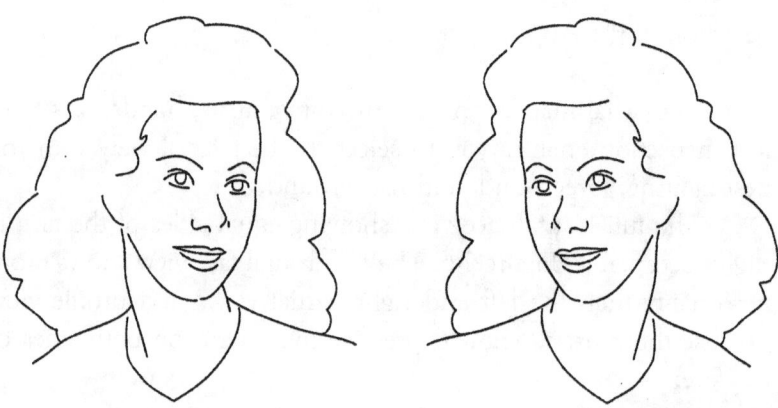

Figure 7-7
Left or Right Partial View

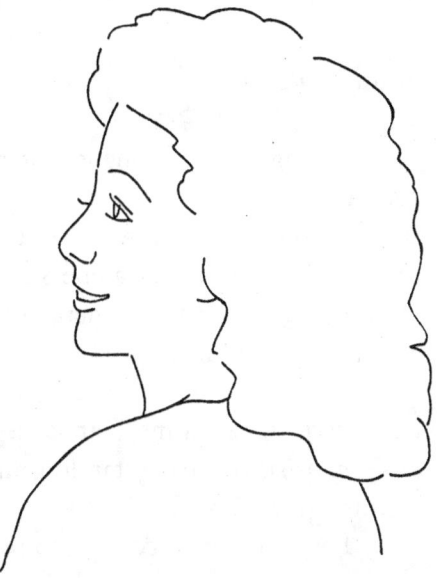

Figure 7-8
Profile View

The profile is "normal" if the forehead, chin, mouth, and jaw are aligned with an imaginary vertical line drawn from the base of frontal bone through the base of the nose, Figure 7-9. The receding or advancing variations of facial features from the imaginary line require positioning the face to emphasize and subdue characteristics.

In the inspection and selection of facial views don't attempt to set absolute measurements. No perfect standard exists in any subject because of the variance in shape, weight, features, color, mental attitudes, and presence. Not only will you photograph subjects with beautiful hair, white teeth, peaches and cream complexion, enchanting eyes, but also those with weak chins, bald spots, crooked noses, and missing teeth.

The variances determine the employment of the Enhancing Techniques listed on pages 127-132.

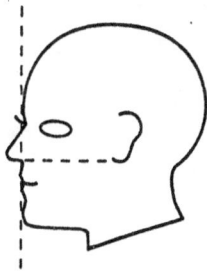

Figure 7-9
Profile Line

Exercise

A good way to practice facial and body inspection is to look at yourself in the mirror in addition to looking at facial and body features of other people. You'll find many people to observe and analyze in television and motion pictures.

The complete inspection of the face, body, and moods aids your appreciation for people and their wonderful differences.

Posing

Defining Posing

Posing is the "tongue" of a non-verbal language quickly communicating to the viewer hundreds of informational pieces such as indifference, arrogance, devotion, happiness, anger, and pride. A sense of self-awareness motivates the pose as the subject knowingly faces the camera under arranged conditions to assimilate a "still life."

As you position your subject, lines of design form with the head, face, torso, arms, hands, legs, and feet. The repertory of poses consists of lifelike standing and seated "stances" with varying gestures.

Posing differs according to regions or cultures, but universal gestures and expressions such as the smile, frown, tilt of the head, and bending of the arms are characteristic of all persons and speak through any era, nation, or culture.

Each subject has his own territory or space around him. The pose protects each subject like a "mask." The subject will only drop his mask to reveal his extraordinary aspects when he doesn't feel the need for the mask. Your special efforts to put your subject at ease will help the subject remove his mask.

The first step in posing places the head with the lighting requirements for the face in the desired general direction of the light. The torso is then aligned according to the head angle. The arms, hands, legs, and feet balance with the face and torso symmetrically or asymmetrically. A small amount of tension is permissible and "stretches the eye."

Defining the Three Classic Poses

The classic standing and seated poses originate at a 45 degree angle to the camera creating a diagonal line of design, Figures 7-10, 7-11.

The three classic poses that reflect the subject's attitude are:
- Head and shoulders pose
- Standing partial and full length pose
- Seated partial and full length pose

These timeless posing elements contain balanced composition, the separating of the subject from the foreground and background, the distribution of weight in the subject's pose, and distribution of the subject's movement.

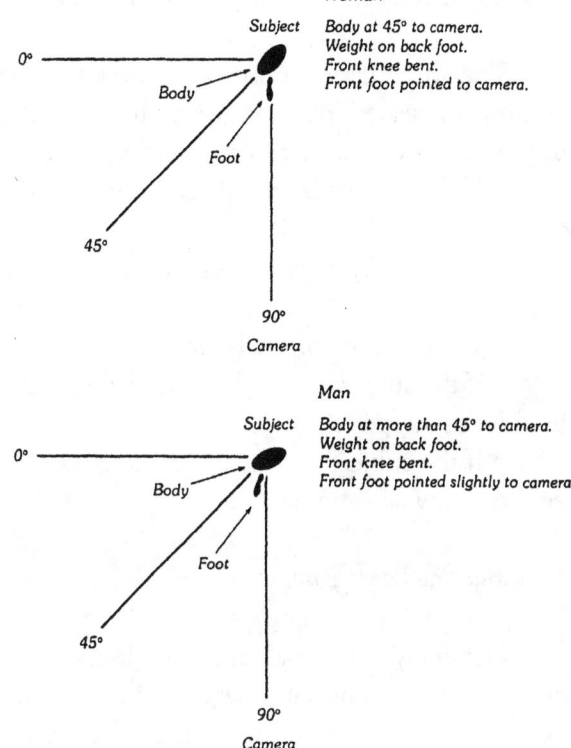

Figure 7-10
Classic Standing Pose Diagram

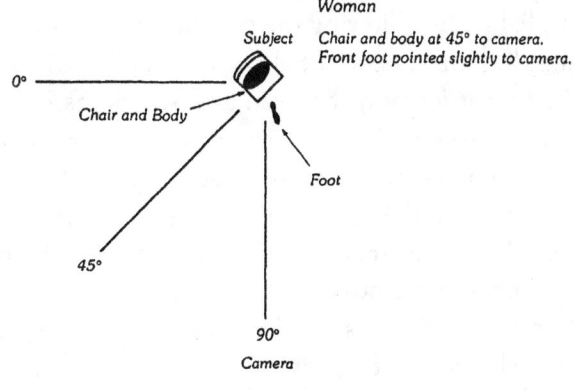

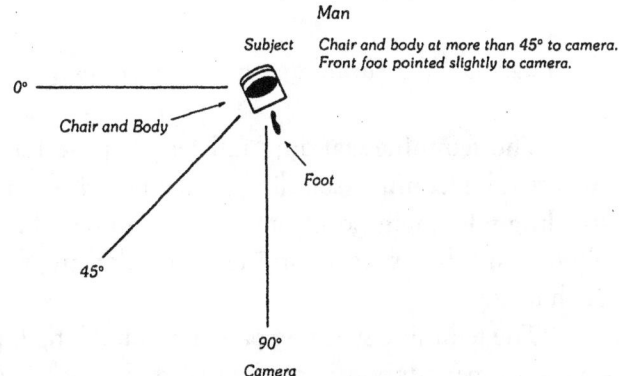

Figure 7-11
Classic Seated Pose Diagram

Defining the Support For the Three Classic Poses

The three classic poses and their variations evolve from a standing or seated position with the lowest point of the most support being the basic posing building block.

• If the subject is standing, the lowest support point is the foot.

• If the subject is seated, the lowest support point is the buttocks.

Two variations of the basic supports:

• If the subject is standing and leaning on a column, use the shoulder as support.

• If the subject is seated and the elbow is resting on a prop, use the elbow as support.

Head and Shoulders Pose

Generally, the head and shoulders pose is made indoors with a studio posing table with main and fill lights to light the subject. The studio posing table is invaluable in head and shoulders work, but is usually missing in outdoor portraiture because the table is awkward to take to outdoor locations.

In outdoor color portraiture the head and shoulders pose is accomplished by following the guidelines for posing the subject in the standing or seated partial or full length pose. Then compose the final print for only the head and shoulders.

The head and shoulders pose positions the head in the upper third of the portrait. The pose includes all of the head, neck, and the top of the shoulder. The portrait extends to a point between the shoulders and elbow according to the line of clothes. The woman's entire bustline isn't included, Figure 7-12.

In the head and shoulders pose the area below the shoulder is free of clutter in the foreground, background, and on the subject unless the clutter serves a special purpose.

Feminine Standing Partial and Full Length Pose

The feminine standing full length pose includes all of the subject. The feminine standing partial pose is created by using the standing full length pose composed to midway between the lower hipline and the knees according to the clothing and placement of the hands.

The feminine standing partial and full length poses are based on the proper support at the lowest level which is the foot.

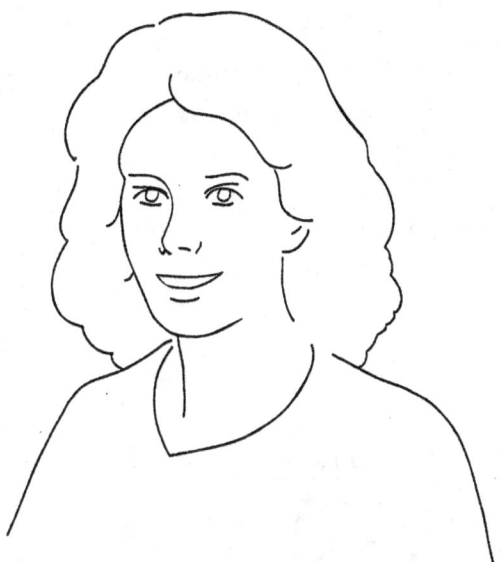

Figure 7-12
Head and Shoulders Pose

The following are guidelines for the feminine standing full length pose, Figure 7-13:

• The feet are separated slightly to distribute weight and form a solid support.

• The subject is placed in a left or right 45 degree angle to the camera to create a front (closest to the camera) and back (farthest from the camera) shoulder. The feminine standing full length pose is seldom less than a 45 degree angle except for a profile or special effect. The angle of the body is not wide enough for the bustline, stomach, and back arm to extend past the contour of the body.

• The subject's weight is on the back foot. This causes the back shoulder to be lower than the front shoulder creating a diagonal line from the front to back shoulder. The diagonal line repeats in the bustline, armline, kneeline, hipline, and footline.

• The body faces the same direction as the face.

• The spine supports the body in an upright position with the back outward curve less than if sitting.

• The front leg is slightly bent at the knee.

• The front foot and toe points toward the camera.

• The subject leans forward slightly from the waist to create a slightly advancing, positive, and "alive" attitude. To lean backwards gives a weak, detached image.

• The top of the head is tilted toward the front shoulder to create a gentle S curve. For an older woman, position the head perpendicular to the body.

• The arm or arms are bent at the elbow to create a diagonal line.

• The elbow is extended slightly away from the body to create space or light between the body and arm, thus creating the effect of a "waist line."

• The hands are placed with one active and one passive at varying heights with one in profile.

• Variations of hands and legs poses are discussed on pages 119-124.

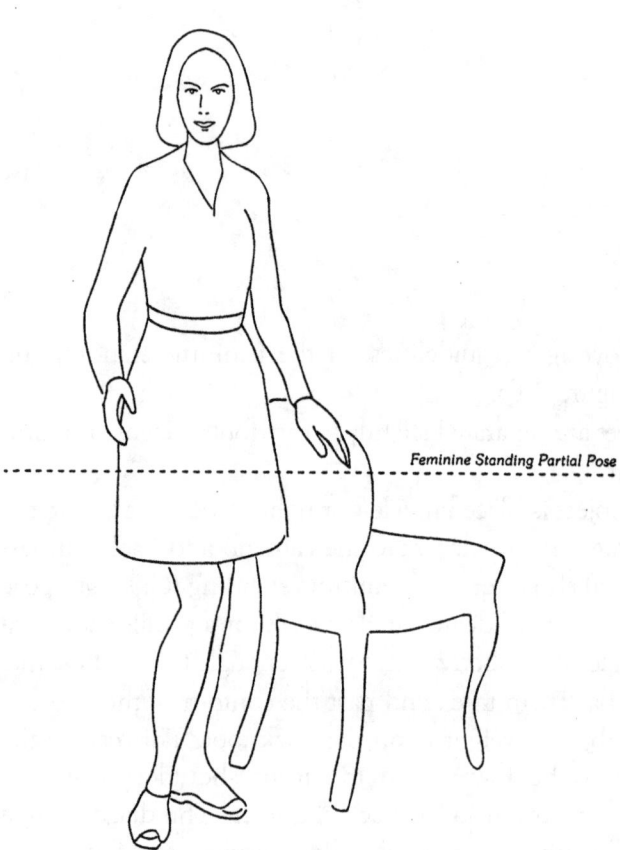

Feminine Standing Partial Pose

Figure 7-13
Feminine Standing Partial and
Full Length Pose

Feminine Seated Partial and Full Length Pose

The feminine seated full length pose includes all of the subject and chair. The feminine seated partial pose is created with the seated full length pose composed below the knees.

The feminine seated pose is based on the proper support at the lowest level which is the buttocks.

The following are guidelines for the feminine seated full length pose, Figure 7-14:

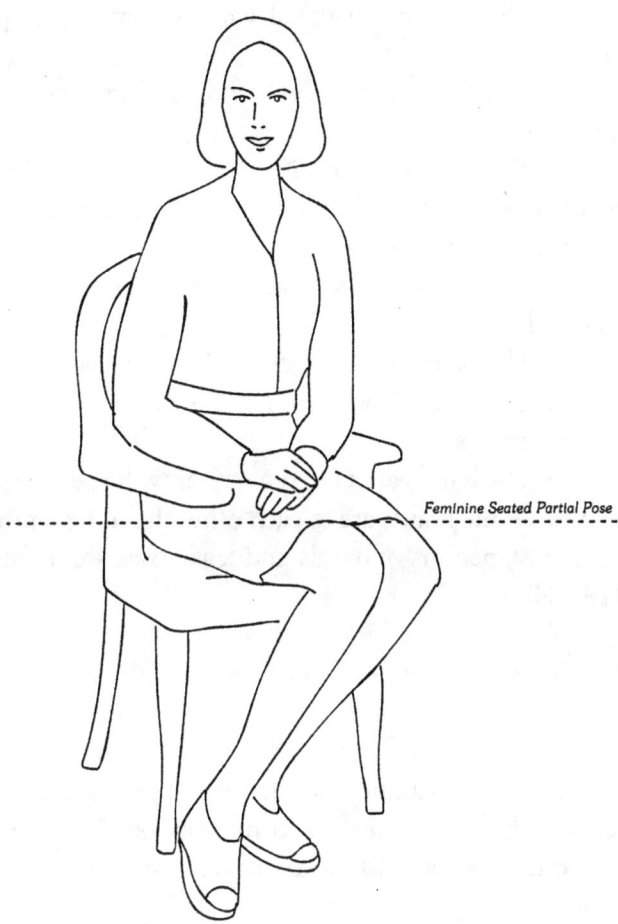

Feminine Seated Partial Pose

Figure 7-14
Feminine Seated Partial and Full
Length Pose

• The subject and chair are placed parallel at a 45 degree angle to the camera.

• The body, face, knees, and feet face the same direction as the chair.

• The subject sits on the front part of the chair to avoid a backward slump by leaning into the back of the chair.

• The weight of the body rests on the back thigh or buttocks.

• The subject leans forward slightly from the waist to present positiveness. If the body leans backwards from the waist the subject appears aloof.

• The spine supports the body in an upright position with the back outward curve more than in a standing position.

• The knees are bent.

• The feet are brought to the side of the front shoulder, almost in line beneath the shoulders.

• The legs are diagonal with the front foot pointed at the camera.

• The back foot remains at a 45 degree angle with the heel lifted slightly.

• The top of the head is tilted toward the front shoulder to create a gentle S curve. For an older woman, position the head perpendicular to the body.

• The arms are bent at the elbow to create a comfortable diagonal line.

• The bent elbow is extended slightly away from the body to create the effect of a "waist line." This diagonal line also softens the shoulder angle.

• The hands are placed together with the palms up or down. The closer the hands are to each other the more feminine the pose.

• Variations of hands and legs poses are discussed on pages 119-124.

Masculine Standing Partial and Full Length Pose

The masculine standing full length pose includes all of the subject. The masculine standing partial pose is created by using the full length pose composed to midway between the lower hipline and the knees according to the clothing and placement of the hands.

The masculine standing partial and full length pose is based on the proper support at the lowest level which is the foot.

The following are guidelines for the masculine standing full length pose, Figure 7-15:

• The feet are separated slightly to distribute weight and form a solid support. The spread of the feet is slightly more than in the feminine pose.

• The subject is placed in a left or right 45 degree angle to the camera to create a front and back shoulder. The subject turns toward the camera more than in the feminine standing pose to create a squarer, broader shoulder line. The masculine standing pose is seldom less than the 45 degree angle except for a profile or special effect. The angle of the body is not wide enough for the chest, stomach, and arm to extend past the contour of the body.

• The subject's weight is on the back foot. This causes the back shoulder to be lower than the front shoulder creating a diagonal line of design from the front to back shoulder. The diagonal line repeats in the chestline, armline, kneeline, hipline, and footline.

• The body faces the same direction as the face.

• The spine supports the subject in an upright position with the back outward curve less than if sitting.

• The front leg is slightly bent at the knee.

• The front foot slightly faces the camera. The angle is less than the feminine pose.

• The subject leans slightly forward from the waist to create a slightly advancing, positive, and "alive" attitude. To lean backwards gives a weak, detached image.

• The head is perpendicular with the body.

• The arm or arms are bent at the elbow to create a diagonal line.

• The hands are placed with one active and one passive at varying heights. One hand can be in a broad profile.

• Variations of hands and legs poses are discussed on pages 119-124.

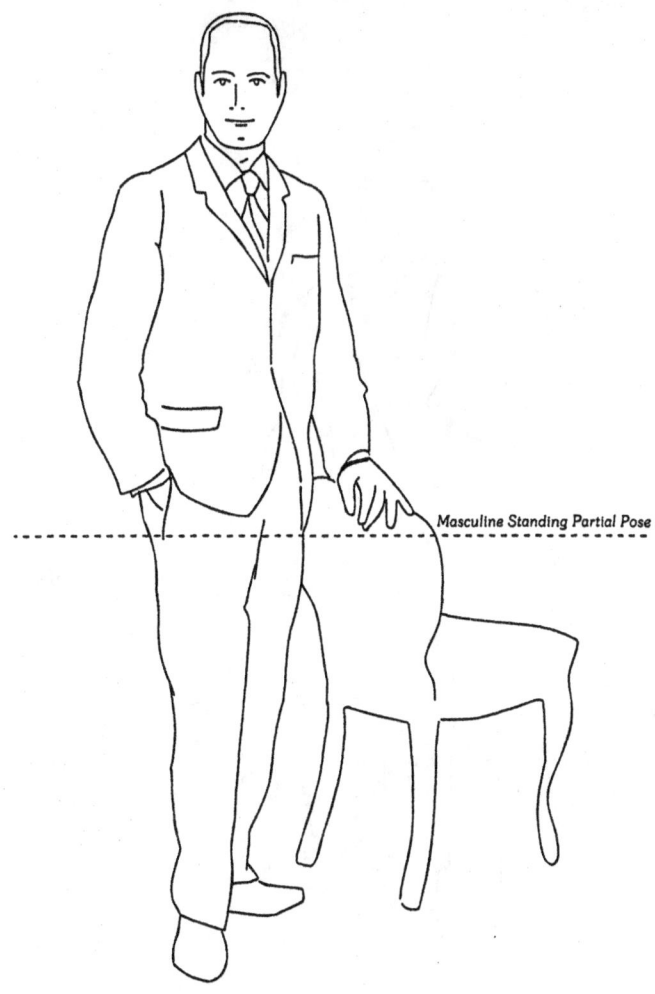

Masculine Standing Partial Pose

Figure 7-15
Masculine Standing Partial and
Full Length Pose

Masculine Seated Partial and Full Length Pose

     The masculine seated full length pose includes all of the subject and chair. The masculine seated partial pose is created with the seated full length pose composed below the knees.

     The masculine seated pose is based on the proper support at the lowest level which is the buttocks.

     The following are guidelines for the masculine seated full length pose, Figure 7-16:

     • The subject and chair are placed parallel at a slightly more than left or right 45 degree angle to the camera.

     • The body, face, knees, and feet face the same direction as the chair.

     • The subject sits on the front part of the chair to avoid a backward slump by leaning into the back of the chair.

     • The weight of the body rests on the back thigh or buttocks.

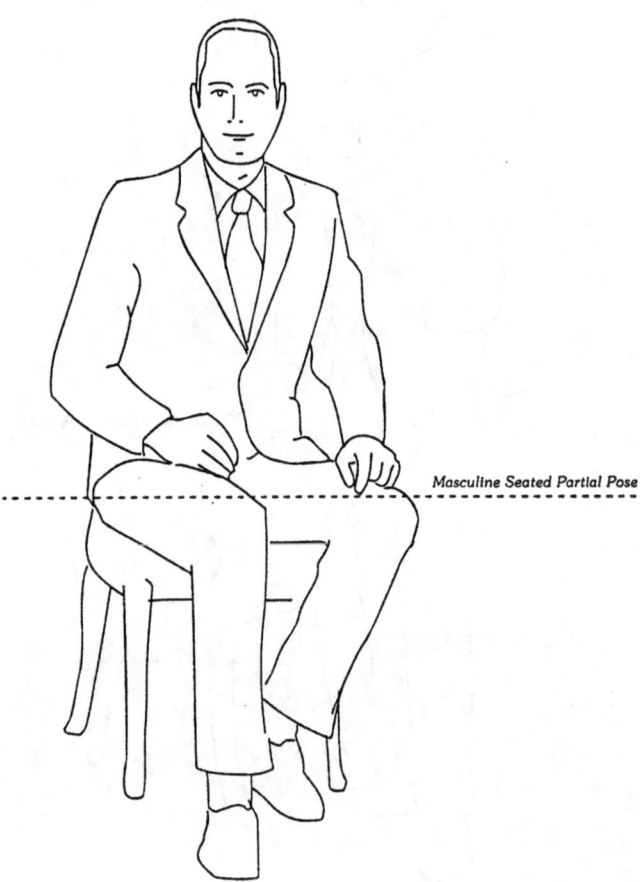

Masculine Seated Partial Pose

Figure 7-16
Masculine Seated Partial and
Full Length Pose

• The subject leans forward slightly from the waist to present positiveness. If the subject leans backwards from the waist, the subject appears aloof.

• The spine supports the subject in an upright position with the back outward curve more than in a standing position.

• The knees remain bent at a slightly more than 90 degree angle to create a diagonal line.

• The legs extend forward, with the knees slightly apart, but not enough to reveal the crotch area.

• The front foot points with the same angle as the body.

• Place the back foot back slightly and at the same angle as the body.

• The head is in a perpendicular position. If the head is slightly tilted the tilt is toward the back shoulder.

• The arms are bent at the elbows to create a comfortable diagonal line.

• The hands are one active and one passive and are placed at varying heights. The further apart the hands, the more masculine the appearance.

• The hands are placed on the thighs. If needed, bring the hands closer into the body to make a definite elbow angle. Place each hand at varying distances from the body.

• Fingers are curled into a loose fist position.

• In the seated partial pose, if the subject is seated on a prop such as a chair, stool, box, or fence, the front leg is placed on a short stool. This raises the front leg to avoid a crotch view.

• Variations of hands and legs poses are discussed on pages 119-124.

Posing Variations

Variations in classic posing are made with small movements such as the tilt of the head, position of the torso, arms, elbow, hands, knees, legs, feet, and the facial views. Sharp and severe angles of the lines of design in the subject create tension. The most noticeable tension is in the neck, face, and shoulder area. To relieve the tension, lessen the angle. Not all variations work well with each subject, but visual experience guides you to judge the proper selection.

All the classic variations make the selection of the negative easier in the darkroom.

The following guidelines for the woman, man, two persons, teenage child, child, infant, and groups are adapted to each person's body language.

Woman

The classic line of design for the feminine pose is an S curve.

A woman considers size more important than a man. (There are few women who don't want to look thinner.) To minimize size in the heavy or chubby woman place more space around her, select dark clothes with a touch of color at the neckline, and place the lighting source at the woman's back.

In a younger woman, an extra touch of vitality is added by the subject tilting the top of her head to the front shoulder. However, in the older, mature, or heavier woman, place the head in a perpendicular position to the body. Allow your experienced eye to determine the head pose rather than let the subject state her age and/or overweight condition.

Pose a woman in slacks with her knees together to avoid the crotch area.

Avoid photographing the armpit area.

Avoid photographing straight into the shoulder because this creates tension lines in the neck when the head is turned to the camera.

A woman's eyes are more glamorous if her eyes look up. In many of the Hollywood glamour portraits of the 1930s, 1940s, and 1950s, the woman's eyes looked up. In the Hollywood publicity portraits glamour was a manufactured product selling dreams and escapism. The subject's eyes hinted at intimacy yet glamour existed in the image not in the person. Glamour is not to be confused with beauty, elegance, or grace. Glamour dictates that the artificial is appreciated and enhanced with the invention of the camera.

A woman's hand is used in a natural function. A standing woman holding a bouquet, purse, or scarf in front of her, gently rests one or both forearms on the front of her hip bone to create an elevated fig leaf position, Figure 7-17. This is particularly good for brides holding a bouquet because the dress is hidden if the bouquet is held too high and awkward if held too low.

When a woman places her hand in a pocket, the open hand rests lightly flat against the body because a fist inside the pocket creates an unsightly line of design.

Avoid a woman posing with her bent arm on a prop that is too high such as a chair or table top. This creates an awkward arm angle and raises the shoulder level.

To conceal a woman's hipline in the standing pose, the front hand is placed on the hip with the narrow profile of the hand resting on the largest part of the hips, Figure 7-18.

To narrow a woman's wide hips, the body is angled to the camera, weight on the back foot, the front knee bent and pointing forward, and the shoulders are square to the camera.

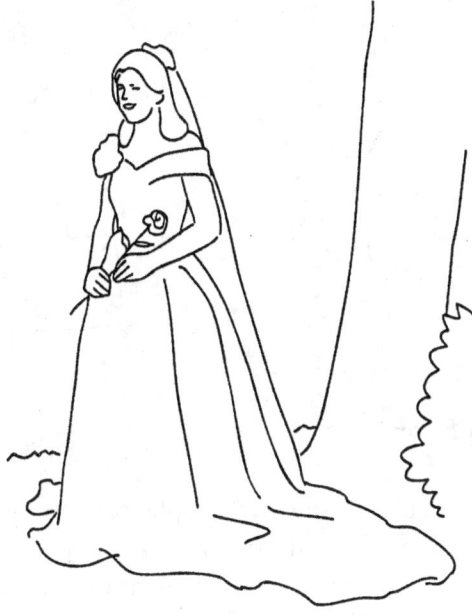

Figure 7-17
Feminine Hand Position
Holding Prop

Man

The classic line of design for the masculine pose is the straight line.

Society dictates that the man look large, aggressive, and angular. At the same time, the male pose should show strength, grace, and a stable presence.

The pose of the man's head in the seated or standing man is perpendicular to the body.

Place the man toward the light source for a broad shoulder appearance.

Use dark clothes with color in the tie if the man's physique is heavy.

A man's arm looks more masculine if the elbow is not bent less than a 90 degree angle. Any time the man's arm is bent less than 90 degrees upward toward the face, the pose appears more feminine, Figure 7-19.

If a man wears a hat, tip the hat back slightly to avoid hiding the face.

When a man places his hand in a suit or pants pocket, the open hand rests lightly flat against the body because a fist inside the pocket creates an unsightly line of design.

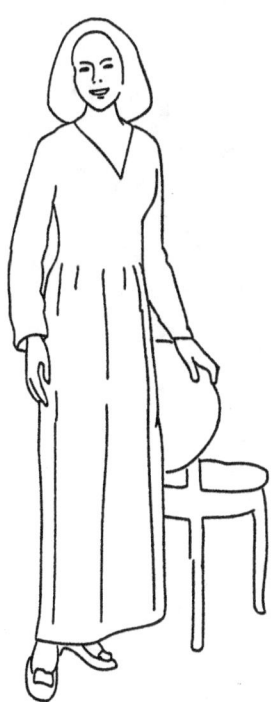

Figure 7-18
Standing Pose to Conceal
Feminine Hipline

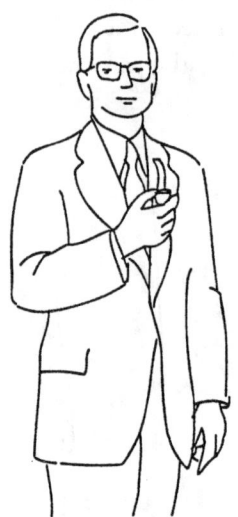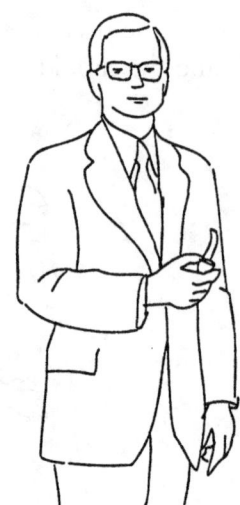

Figure 7-19
Angle of Masculine Bent Elbow

Two Persons

When posing two people together the bigger or taller person commands the authority. In general, pose the two people with the eyebrow of one person at the chin level of the other person. This brings them into a "closeness" particularly if there is a great difference in their seated or standing height.

If the two people are husband and wife or bride-to-be and groom-to-be, blend them together in the pose. Pose the woman first in a pose that functions by itself. Then pose the man to blend into the woman's pose. The man appears dominant if closest to the camera. Be sure to watch for unwanted shadows falling from one person to another.

Teenage Child

The key to posing a teenager is for a teenager to know you accept his youthfulness and his clothes with slight modification.

Dental braces are acknowledged. If keeping the lips in contact to hide the braces looks uncomfortable, don't influence the smile.

Pimples and acne are camouflaged with make-up applied by the teenager or parent. (You want to avoid any responsibility of an allergic reaction.) Negative retouching is another solution.

Child

A child poses basically the same as a man and woman. A child who is old enough to follow directions is posed by gentle guidance. The child provides natural spontaneity, exaggerated action, and direct honesty that isn't suppressed, but managed.

A child shouldn't be over posed or overproped to conform to a preconceived idea that a child only embodies a miniature adult. In reality, a child is an entity unto himself. If you feel you have to exert total control, you shouldn't attempt to photograph a child.

A small child in a portrait with an adult is arranged by bringing the child up to the adult level or by moving the adult down to the child's level.

In a portrait a small child occupies less image space than the image space allowed for adults.

The fine line between a formal portrait and "candid" of a child depends on where and how the child looks. The photograph becomes more of a portrait when the child looks at the camera. A formal portrait and a candid is further distinguished by how the child looks into the camera and sees you. If the child looks into the camera, sees you as a person rather than a portraitist, more candid emotion is produced. If the child realizes you sense he has feelings this eliminates any intimidation.

Observe the child for shyness or outgoing qualities. A talkative, outgoing child permits you to interact with conversation, but remain cautious because too much stimulation can create havoc! A shy, reserved child is best approached by first talking to the parent then transferring the conversation gradually to the child. Talk reservedly to the shy child and wait for the child to come forward and get involved. To retain control of a shy or outgoing child you must choose to accommodate the child by acting shy or outgoing.

Avoid harsh commands when directing a child. A soft voice, even a whisper, has a soothing effect on a child.

Whether photographing an outgoing or a shy child, save one or two exposures for after the creative session in case the child makes an unexpected pose or expression.

In photographing a female child with average physique, use the feminine pose with tilted head or the masculine perpendicular head pose. A child with a heavy or chubby physique looks best with the masculine perpendicular head pose. Allow your experienced eye to determine the pose rather than your calling attention to the subject's weight.

Maintain the camera in a fixed position with the latitude a remote control cord provides or with a hand held camera in a less fixed position.

To aid in posing bring a toy or ask the child to bring a toy to use as a prop, arouse the child's interest, and increase his attention span.

For a small child you need to get on your knees to work at the child's level. Avoid tilting the camera down or a grassy ground may form the background.

Focus on the subject is critical because children are seldom still. The best aperture setting includes more depth of field.

Infant

Until an infant holds up his head he is photographed lying on his back or sitting in an infant seat. The first choice of clothing is a solid color. Use a non-patterned background.

A slant board covered with a fabric for a background is useful in propping up the infant. Direct the infant's eye by using an overhead mobile or toy. A small toy is placed in one hand to interest him.

An additional pose is for a parent to sit in a chair, hold the infant on his back in the parent's extended arms. This allows the infant to look at the parent for meaningful eye contact.

If the infant can hold up his head, the stomach position is easily used. In this position, the infant raises his head, supports his weight on his bent elbows, and looks at the camera. To direct the infant's interest, place an object nearby.

Groups

An assemblage of people who are related in any way is considered a group.

A group portrait works well when a number of people congregate to establish a group identity. An individual portrait allows a person his identity and image of himself. A group portrait removes that individuality and is replaced with a "group identity." The idea that a person belongs to a group is so important that a single individual doesn't mind losing his identity for a short time. At first glance, the viewer sees the group as a whole, but later each person emerges.

The pose sets the portrait's overall mood. Vertical lines of standing people set a formal mood. If the people are seated, the mood becomes casual.

The most photographed group is the family and consists of one or more generations. Often the portrait is a once-in-a-lifetime occasion. Group family portraits tell more than who is in the portrait because it gives clues to the social history of the family, the emotional relationships in the family, and the environment tells of their economic status. Over the lifetime of a family, patterns develop as to who stands next to whom, how family members touch, expressions, who stays at the side, the gaps of separateness, the boys more prominent than the girls or vice versa.

The family offers a variety of ages and sizes with which to work. There are many different sets of eyes for you to see such as the mother, father, and children, but when all these eyes look at you, all they see is the camera's eye.

There are several types of group compositions:
- Straight Line Group
- Instinctive Group
- Major and Minor Group
- Triangle Group
- Cluster Group
- Free-form Group

Whatever the approach, you build a common link or similar pattern between the people, such as having the group looking the same direction, touching one another, or any active or passive cooperative gesture.

The following are a few guidelines for group composition:

Straight Line Group

A person in a Straight Line Group loses his individuality as the viewer's eye moves quickly with little interest across each straight line or row. If a row situation is unavoidable, place the rows where each person's face is on a different level. No face should be immediately above another face. Place the taller people in the back row with the average heights in the middle row, and the shorter heights in the front row. The width of each row is varied, and the end of each row curves gently toward the camera to form an S curve.

In very large groups, a row behind the tallest is made by standing people on benches or the equivalent. If the setting has an incline or stairs the rows are diagonal. The lower supporting base row should appear heavier than the upper rows. To avoid harsh shadows on the face, place the group in open shade.

A group presents the hazard of many blinking eyes, requiring numerous exposures. When selecting the first previews, count the number of people blinking and eliminate the previews with the most blinking eyes.

Use a remote control cord because the group responds favorably to your instructions when you can look at the group.

Instinctive Group

The Instinctive Group gathers in your chosen setting and, usually, the group forms spontaneously. Best friends congregate, families group, and if a company portrait, the directors and employees group accordingly. After the initial grouping, your responsibility is to direct the lines of design, facial and body posing, and use the proper lighting.

Major and Minor Group

In the Major and Minor Group, the major person receives the easily read left to right position and first choice in clothing color. The minor person receives a secondary position balancing the major's position. These major and minor positions are determined by seniority, sibling rivalry, and in a family, the mother and father.

In a family, the mother becomes the "major," the father the "minor." Seat the mother on the left, facing right leaning slightly inward towards the group because the viewer's eye sees the mother first and travels easily left to right. The father is standing to the right and back of the mother. If there is no father, place the tallest child in this position to balance the portrait. Add other members, equally apart, overlapping, balancing heights, sizes, and colors of clothes. Create different levels using stools, chairs, benches, and the ground. Tilt heads subtly into the center of the portrait. Allow each individual a different activity with his hands. Use open-shade lighting to eliminate harsh shadows, Figure 7-20.

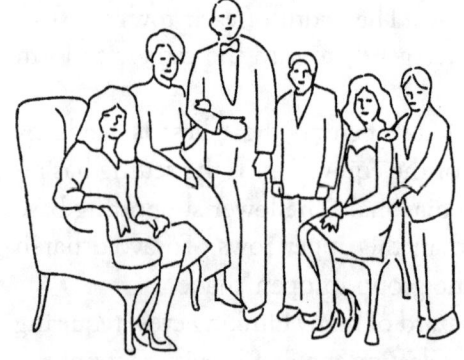

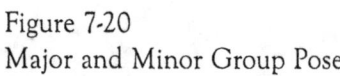
Figure 7-20
Major and Minor Group Pose

Triangle Group

A symmetrical triangle has a defined, strong, clear edge of straight lines and sets a formal mood. A triangle of irregular edges is asymmetrical and less formal.

A triangle group portrait places one shorter row of persons behind a longer row of persons with all the faces at different levels. The base forms the heaviest line, and the top the lightest line. The larger the group, the larger the base line. The face highest in the format becomes the most important focal point. Even-numbered groups of people are easiest to work with because they divide easily into rows, Figure 7-21.

In the triangle the two people in the two outside positions of the base line add strength to the entire base line. By facing the people outward, the base line is broadened. If the outside position of the triangle base line is a woman, place her at the end of the row with her body, legs, and feet turned outward to avoid a hipline. Extend the woman's legs outward at a low angle with the front leg extended further out by placing the back knee higher than the front knee. If the outside position of the triangle base line is a man, place the man at the end of the row with his body, legs, and feet turned outward. Extend the man's legs at a 45 degree angle. The back leg is extended further out by placing the front knee higher than the back knee, Figure 7-22.

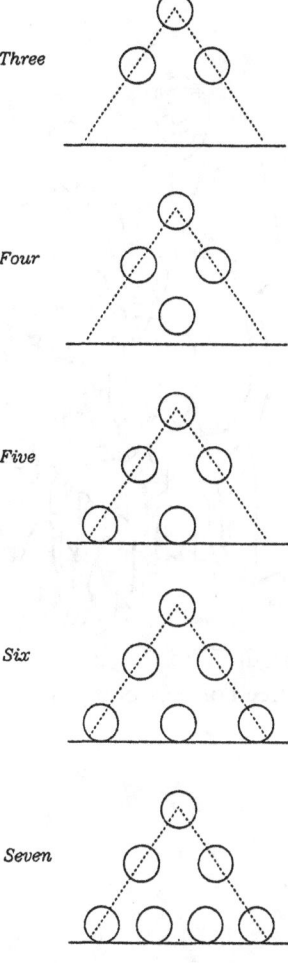

Three

Four

Five

Six

Seven

Figure 7-21
Triangle Group Diagram

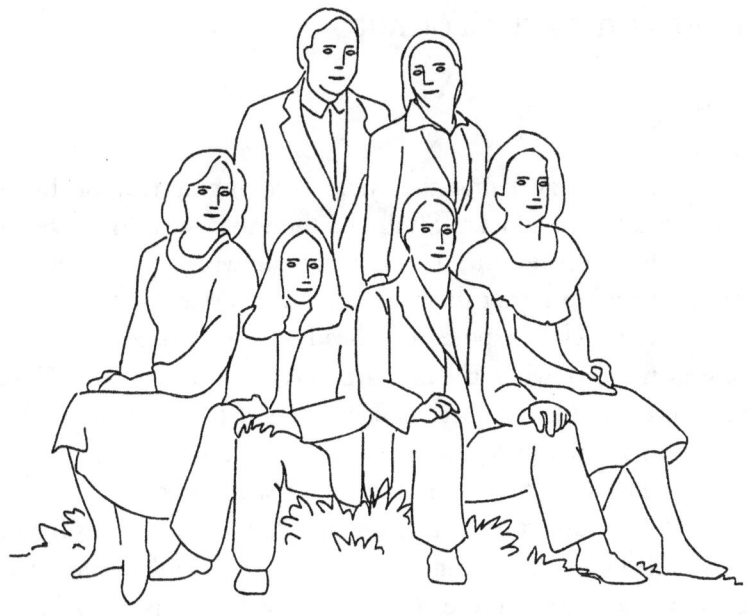

Figure 7-22
Triangle Group Pose

Cluster Group

A cluster of people results when they are divided into sub-groups. Each sub-group offers a portrait that functions alone if removed from the larger group portrait.

A four-generation family portrait is broken into four sub-groups with each subgroup representing a family. Or, the four-generation family portrait is broken into parents, children, all women, mothers and daughters, and fathers and sons.

In a corporation, the officers, board of directors, and employees are subgrouped.

Each subgrouping is color co-ordinated which blends with the overall color of the portrait.

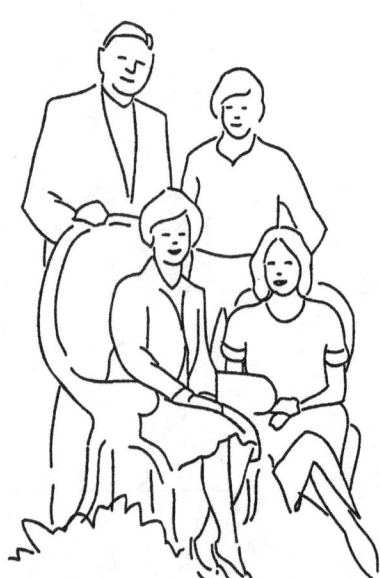

Figure 7-23
Free Form Group Pose

Free-form Group

Free-form combines the angles and straight lines of the triangle group form and the smooth, free flow of the major and minor form.

The rigidity of the triangle relaxes to a spontaneous curving rhythmic line of arrested movement. The major and minor grouping of assigned places relaxes. Heads are at the same level, but not directly next to each other.

A larger triangle is formed with the faces and includes several overlapping smaller triangles. The lines of design move the eye gently through the portrait, Figure 7-23.

Fine Tuning the Portrait

Eyes

In everyday living the most meaningful relationships are direct eye to eye contact. Similarly, the most meaningful portraits are with direct eye to eye contact allowing a natural, direct communication rather than distant and assumed.

In the classic pose, the head and eyes face in the same direction except when the eyes are looking at the camera. The eyes are centered unless a special effect is desired.

There are options for the subject's eyes:

• The subject looks at the viewer with direct eye contact.

• The subject looks into the distance which implies the mind is occupied with something of which the viewer isn't aware. Looking into the distance with eyes looking down is a pensive look.

• The subject looks at a task he is performing and the viewer is aware of the subject's activity.

Larger opening of the pupils gives more personality to the eyes. An electronic strobe opens up the pupils slightly to create a more personable look.

Eyes have a tendency to be swollen in the early morning hours. Photograph an older man or woman in the afternoon to avoid swollen eyes.

To avoid a "stare look," ask the subject to move his eyes often by glancing around.

The problem of eye blinking is solved in several ways:

• Have the subject blink purposely after each exposure to establish an acceptable rhythm.

• Have the subject close his eyes for a few moments and allow the eyelids to absorb the lighting.

• Tap on the tripod to make a noise causing the subject to blink before the exposure is made.

• Have the subject blink several times before the exposure.

A "catchlight" is a sparkle of light reflecting the light source into the iris of the eye. The catchlight is on the same side as the originating direction of the light source. The need for a catchlight is debatable. The correct placing of the studio main light will result in a catchlight. To obtain the best catchlights in the studio, direct the main light from the front and one side approximately 45 degrees to the subject and camera, and from above the subject's head.

The ideal place for a catchlight is in the iris of the eye between 10 A.M. and 2 P.M. positions. There should be only one catchlight per eye. Two catchlights create a flickering appearance, Figure 7-24.

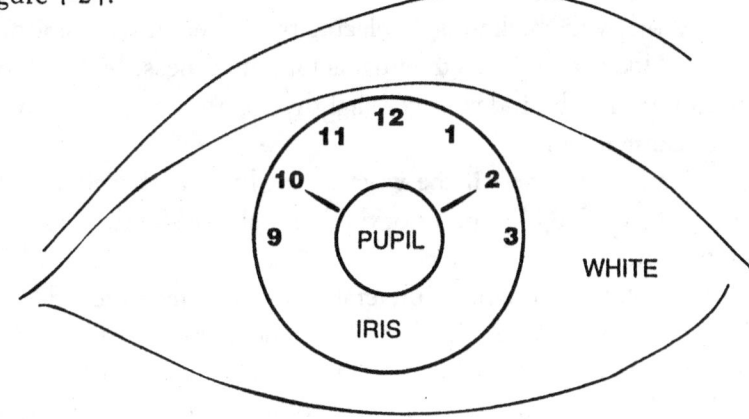

Figure 7-24
Catchlights

Arms

Arms crossed hugging the body closely or tightly indicate defensiveness. Arms crossed openly or casually extended from the body represent openness.

Elbows bent and arms extended forward from the waist appear larger, more if the arm is bare.

Hands

Hands represent a small part of the person but act as a barometer for the entire person.

Body language, not an exact science, includes the hands such as clenched fists indicating pressure and anxiety. Holding both hands behind the back means superiority, and hands upright in a "praying position" relates smugness. Always place the hand in a position where the hand gesture looks neither vague, forced, flabby, or uncertain.

In a portrait the hands are a compliment to the whole image and aren't singled out purposely. If hands are attractive show them in a minor way and if unattractive, subdue them in a low light or shadow.

With both feminine and masculine hand poses, show one hand active and one hand passive. The hand closest to the camera is the prominent, active hand. The hand farthest from the camera is the less prominent, passive hand.

If the hands are posed together pose the less prominent, farthest hand from the camera first, then pose the most prominent, closest hand to the camera.

Hands add interest if not held at the same level. If one hand is in a pocket or on the hip, place the other hand at another level.

Don't compose by cutting off the hand in the middle of the hand.

Work with the hands by placing the fingers into position. A flat hand looks rigid. Curl the fingers for naturalness. Make a loose fist and extend the index finger slightly but not pointingly. Avoid interlocking fingers.

Hands look best if the wrist is not broken sharply in a 90 degree angle. The high point of the hand should be the wrist and not the knuckle.

An elongated hand is preferable to one foreshortened.

Place the hands close to the same plane as the face. A maximum of eighteen inches is an allowable distance from the face, the less the better. If the hands are too far in front or back of the subject, the hands appear distorted.

The thumb is not as graceful as the little finger.

Avoid photographing the palms of the hands.

If props are held in the hands, the subject holds the props lightly, not tightly.

Don't call attention to the hands because once the subject becomes aware of his hands, he has difficulty relaxing them.

If the hands begin to appear stiff during a session, ask the subject to shake his hands to relax them. Then repose them with a minimum of instructions.

Woman

A woman's hand looks best in profile with the index finger and thumb forming a "V" shape, Figure 7-25.

Place the palm side of the hand on the solid surface with the weight on the heel of the palm. Bend the wrist slightly by pushing the wrist down to make a graceful pose. A "V" shape is formed by the thumb and index finger. Keep the thumb close to the fingers so the thumb doesn't appear to be hanging. The thumb is slightly bent and held upwards toward the thumb to form the V. Extend the index finger slightly in an arc. Keep the two center fingers together. Keep the little finger relaxed.

If the hands are touching the face, place the hand in an upward position with the hand or fingers lightly touching the face.

When hands are posed above the waist, the fingers are extended upward. When posing two hands above the waist, place one hand higher than the other to lengthen the hand area. Hands posed below the waist are posed downward.

When placing the woman's hand in a hipline pocket, place the hand to show at mid-palm.

If a hand hangs by the side of the body, curl three fingers and place the thumb and index finger to point down and form a V.

In a standing position, if the arm is at the side of the body and if the wrist bends, the wrist bends into the body.

In holding a bridal bouquet, the less prominent hand or hand futherest from the camera holds the bouquet steady. The prominent or hand closest to the camera is in profile.

Additional feminine hand poses are shown in two Figures 7-26.

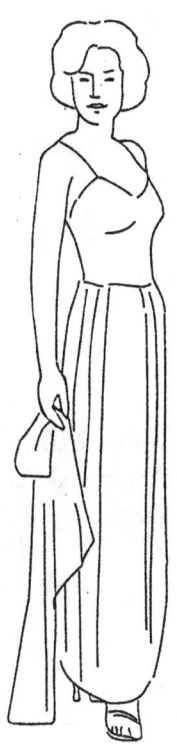

Figure 7-25
Feminine Hand in Profile with
a "V"

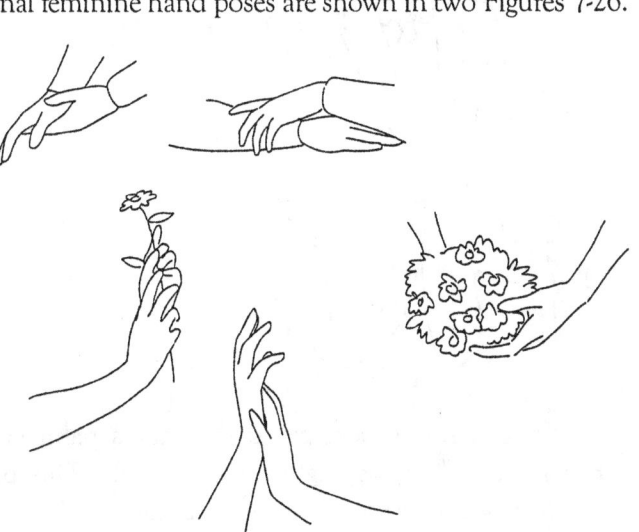

Figure 7-26
Additional Feminine Hand
Poses

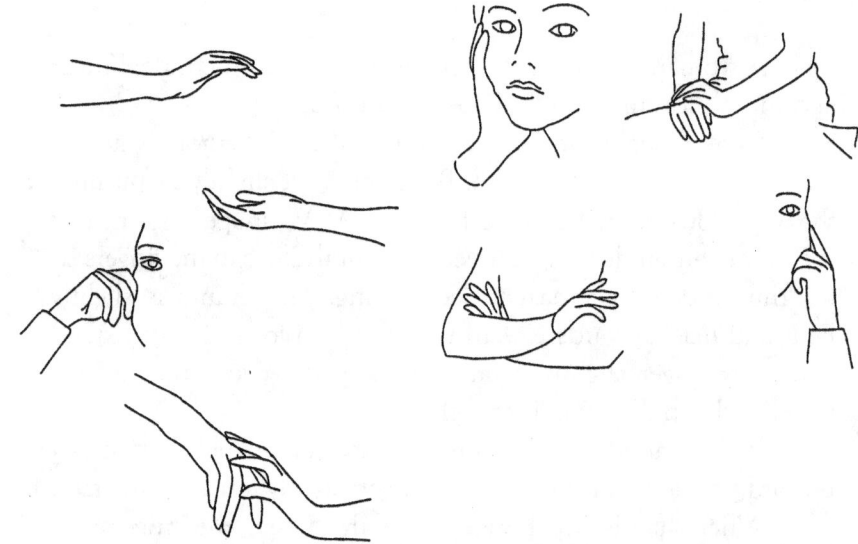

Figure 7-26
Additional Feminine Hand
Poses

Man

A man's hand looks best when in broad profile with the
fingers and thumb gently curved to form a "V," Figure 7-27.

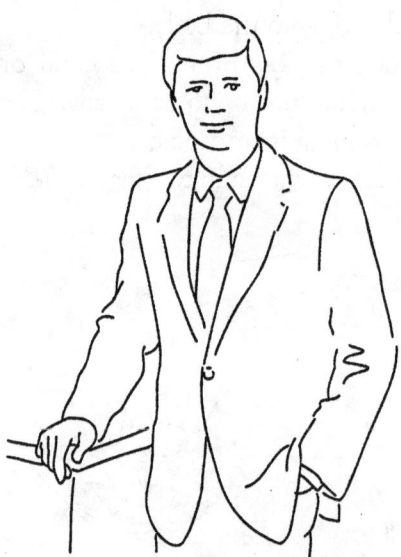

Figure 7-27
Masculine Hand In Broad
Profile With a "V"

In a standing pose avoid the man's palm facing the front
when his arm hangs straight down his side. This position causes
the forearm to angle away from the body.

In a standing pose a man's hands look good at his side with
one hand passive and the other hand active by holding something
or having a function.

All hands look best when placed on a background free of confusion, such as patterns and shadows.

Avoid placing the hands in a fig leaf pose.

When a man places his hand on the shoulder of another person the fingertips should be placed lightly on the shoulders.

Place a man's jewelry such as a watch or identification bracelet on his wrist to show only the edge of the jewelry.

Additional masculine hand poses are shown in Figure 7-28.

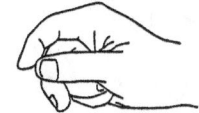
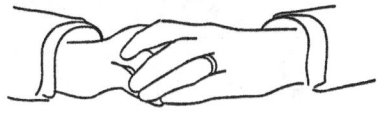
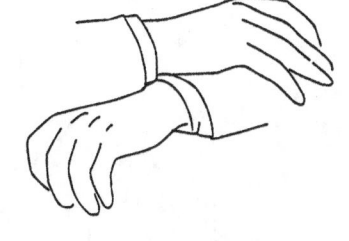
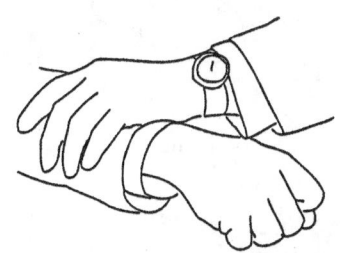

Figure 7-28
Additional Masculine Hand
Poses

Legs

The foot is almost the lowest point of the most support for the subject. The legs are the first extension of the foot and are treated as a viable part of the pose. Legs aren't as much of a barometer of body language as the hands; but if the legs are posed poorly, they detract from the portrait. If posed properly the leg is attractive and adds to the portrait.

Extend the legs only about eighteen inches in front or back of the subject to prevent distortion of the legs.

In a standing feminine or masculine pose, when leaning with the upper part of the body against a tree or column, if the legs are crossed, the leg closest to the column or tree is crossed over the farthest leg from the tree or column. This throws the subject's weight into the column or tree to balance the body, Figure 7-29.

Woman

A woman's leg looks more feminine in a high heel shoe because it adds length, grace, and sensuality to the form.

A woman's leg appears narrower when side lighted.

A standing pose for the younger woman is placing the weight on her back foot, slide the front foot forward bending her knee, roll the knee in slightly, turn toe outward, toe on inside edge, roll ankle in, little toe side carries no weight, Figure 7-30.

Man

A standing man's legs are spread no wider than his shoulder width.

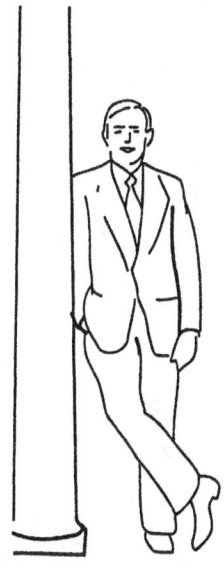

Figure 7-29
Leaning on a Column Pose

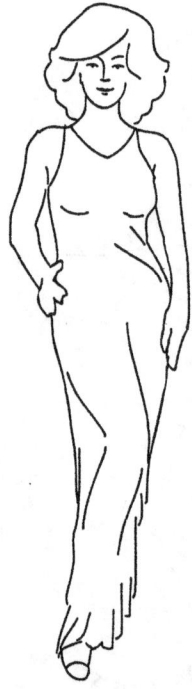

Figure 7-30
Feminine Leg Pose
with Toe Rolled In

Figure 7-31
Subject Posing With
One Foot on Wall

Feet

The feet are the lowest point of the most support for the subject.

When the subject is standing or seated in a 45 degree angle or less to the camera, the front foot points to the camera and blocks the arch of the back foot. This simplifies the lines of design.

If the subject is posed against a wall with one foot placed on the wall, use only the heel on the wall, keeping the toe on the ground, Figure 7-31.

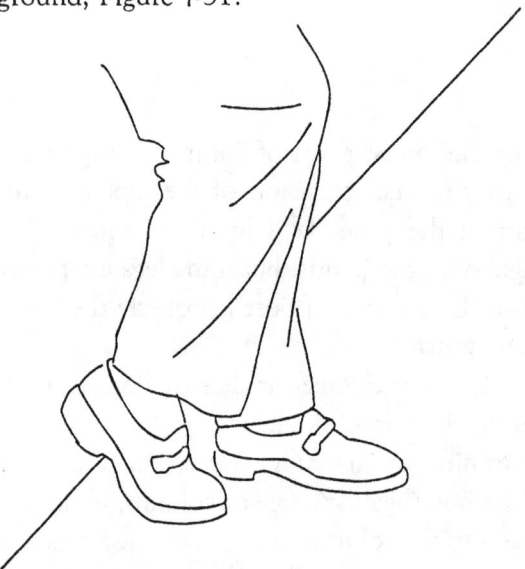

Ground

The ground is an integrated part of the foreground and background and establishes the foundation support for the entire portrait.

The ground can remain as nature intended with all its slopes, curves, and textures. Or, as a result of the lawnmower being invented in the 19th century, the ground can show the results of nature meeting industry, and appear manicured.

Adults and children posing on the ground leads to an informal, casual, clothes selection.

Classic ground poses:
• Subject seated on the ground
  Feminine
  Masculine
• Masculine kneeling on the ground

It's an advantage to demonstrate the pose to the subject by your actually posing on the ground.

The feminine seated pose on the ground, Figure 7-32:

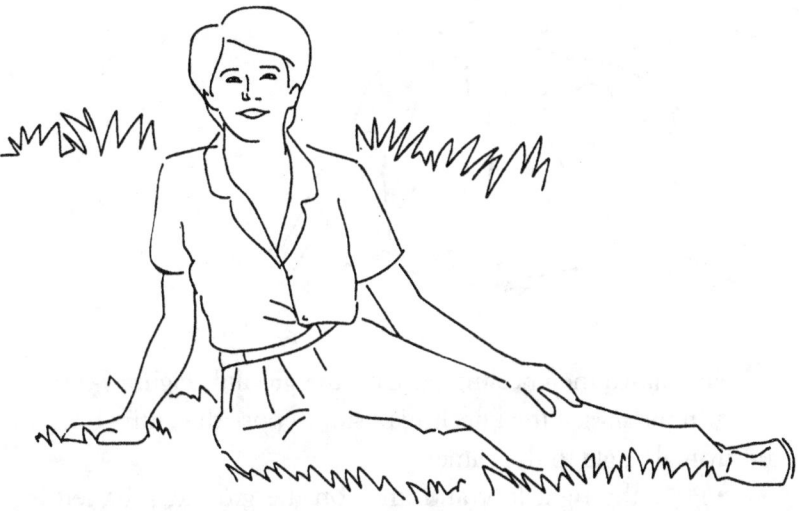

Figure 7-32
Feminine Seated Pose on the
Ground

• In the feminine seated position on the ground, pose the full body at a full frontal angle to the camera.

• Place weight on the right or the left hip. If the right hip holds the weight, place the legs to the left. If the left hip holds the weight, place the legs to the right. The body is supported by the back.

• The top leg always goes forward over the bottom leg to form a narrow line. Point the forward toe.

• The arm opposite the extended legs extends to the ground for balance, not support. The hand on the ground forms a V profile.

• Place the arm on the "raised" hip side with the bent elbow resting on the forward leg.

• The hand crossing over the extended leg is in a V profile.

The masculine seated pose on the ground, Figure 7-33:

• In the masculine seated pose on the ground, pose the full body at a slightly more than 45 degree angle to the camera.

• Place weight on the front buttocks. The back supports the body.

• Extend the legs in the same direction as the body.

• Bend the front knee to extend the leg backwards.

• Bend and raise the back knee to form a diagonal line with the back foot on the ground.

• Extend the arm opposite the legs to the ground for balance. The hand is flat on the ground with the hand in a V profile.

• Extend the arm next to the legs by resting the arm near the elbow on the raised knee. The hand is in a broad V profile.

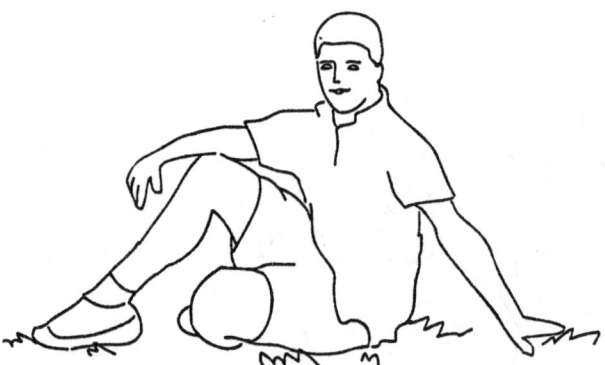

Figure 7-33
Masculine Seated
Pose on the Ground

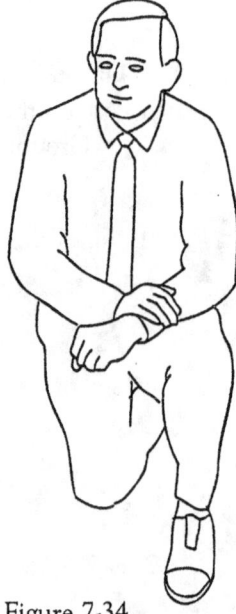

Figure 7-34
Masculine Kneeling
Pose on the Ground

The masculine kneeling pose on the ground, Figure 7-34:

• In the masculine kneeling position, pose the entire body in a full frontal angle to the camera.

• Place the right foot and knee on the ground. The left leg and knee are brought up and forward to a 90 degree angle. With the left elbow at a 90 degree angle, rest the left elbow on the left knee. Keep wrist fairly straight with hand bent slightly. Keep hipline behind subject.

• Bend slightly forward at the waist.

• Bend right elbow. Rest the right hand on the left wrist.

Poses for the man and woman together on the ground are shown in Figure 7-35.

Props

Props support the portrait and are an asset if they don't dominate or detract. Believable props direct and pull the portrait together and introduce symbolism and literalness.

Props add dimension when they are the same color as the background or a subdued color, placed at an angle to the camera, and positioned not to cast a shadow of any consequence.

In using a prop the subject responds differently to each prop such as a high stool, chair, or ground cushion. The subject's response indicates which prop to use.

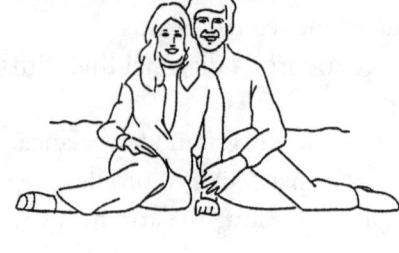
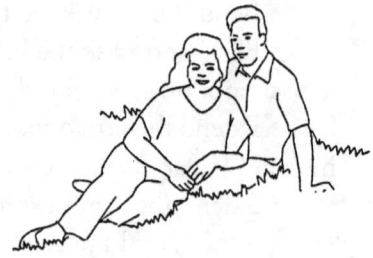

Figure 7-35
Feminine and Masculine
Pose Together on the Ground

Props are hand held or an extension of the ground and add interest if they relate to the subject's interests.

Examples of hand-held props: gloves, cane, fan, parasol, scarf, purse, glasses, hat, rolled-up magazine, flower, bouquet of flowers, tennis racket, golf club, pipe, fishing tackle, and hunting gun.

Examples of props, as an extension of the ground: stool, bench, chair, steps, brick wall, gate, fountain, fence, statue, lawn furniture, large rock, fallen log, mossy spot, pile of leaves, and artificial greenery in a clay pot.

The manner in which a prop is held is directly related to the size and weight of the object. Example: to pick up a pencil requires only two fingers; to pick up a book requires more fingers. A more natural pose results when the subject picks up the prop rather than your handing him the prop. In general, the subject holds the prop lightly, not tightly.

A bouquet of flowers is held high near the neck, midway at the bust line, or at an elevated "fig leaf" level. If the bouquet is held high or midway, touch the bouquet with the front hand using the second center finger to touch the bouquet.

An appropriate height for a chair prop is when the subject sits in the chair the buttocks are higher than the knee.

A subject in a highly stuffed chair or sofa sits forward on the chair or sofa for a firmer base and to avoid sinking.

Enhancing Techniques

Your primary aim is to photograph the subject with a realistic likeness and aesthetic representation. The following is a list of enhancing techniques:

Round Head:
>   Use left or right partial face view.
>   Use camera at eye level.
>   Use short lighting.

Narrow Head:
>   Shadow part of forehead.
>   Use broad lighting.
>   Use camera at high level.
>   Smiles with or without open mouth broaden the face.

Triangular Head:
>   Use camera at low level.
>   Use full frontal face view.

Square Head:
>   Use camera at high level.
>   Use left or right partial face view.

Use short lighting.
Uncomfortable Head Position:
   Move head to left or right position for 10-15 seconds.
Correct Head Position:
   Move head both ways until center of gravity centers the head.
Facial Defects:
   Use split lighting.
   Put defects in shadow area.
Broad Jaw:
   Use left or right partial face view.
   Have subject smile because this makes broad jaw appear oval
      shaped.
High Forehead Plane:
   Use low camera level.
   Tilt chin up.
Broad Forehead Plane:
   Use left or right partial face view.
   Use high camera level.
Receding Forehead Plane:
   Use soft lighting.
   Use full frontal face view.
Elongated Neck:
   Use full frontal face view.
   Head tilted forward.
   Use high camera level.
Short Neck:
   Use left or right partial face view.
Wrinkled Neck:
   Use full frontal face view.
   Use high camera level.
Neck Skin Hanging Over Shirt Collar:
   Turn head away from hanging skin.
Large Adam's Apple:
   Use full frontal face view.
   Head tilted forward.
   Use high camera level.
Wrinkles:
   Use less contrast lighting.
   Use left or right partial face view.
Skin Problems:
   Use soft lighting and soft focus.
Protruding Eyes:
   Have subject look downward.
   Use high camera level.

Deep Set Eyes:
>   Use fill lighting.
>   Use less contrast lighting.
>   Use lower lighting.

Dark Eyes:
>   Use soft lighting.

Small Eyes:
>   Use left or right partial face view.
>   Use low camera level.
>   Head bent forward.
>   Position eyes straight to the front.

Large eyes:
>   Use full frontal face view.
>   Position eyes straight into camera.

Crossed Eyes:
>   Have subject face camera and look in all directions. Find the least problematic angle.

Drooping Eyelids:
>   Have subject look up without moving head up. Then lower eyes, the eyelids will follow but at a slower speed. Do this several times to establish the pattern before making exposure.

Drifting Eye:
>   Establish the pattern of when and how the eye drifts horizontally or vertically. After several observations the drift can be determined. Make exposure at time the eyes are in alignment.

Rapid Oscillation of the eye:
>   Determine the position of the least oscillation by having the subject look in different direction. If there is no position, then use a fast exposure and the law of averages will produce one good exposure.

Cross Eyes:
>   Have subject look at a distant point.
>   Make exposure when eyes are straight.
>   Make a profile view.

Differences in Eyes:
>   Place smaller eye nearer to camera.

Narrow Eye Opening:
>   Use high camera level, then find best level for full eye opening.
>   Have subject lean forward.
>   Have subject blink deliberately and sharply as eyes are open widest after a blink.

One Eye Larger:

     Have subject smile because this causes eyes to close and not be so noticeable.

Eyeglass Reflections:

     Have subject look at dark object.

     Tilt glasses downward.

     Lower or raise chin.

     Use side lighting.

     Tilt the head down slightly.

     Have a reflection-free coating put on eyeglass lens.

Tinted Eyeglasses:

     Inform subject of how the tint alters eye and surrounding skin color.

Prominent Ears:

     Hide back ear behind the head in partial view.

     Keep near ear in shadow.

     Consider a profile view.

     Use high camera level.

Narrow Chin:

     Tilt chin upward.

     Use left or right partial face view.

Prominent Chin:

     Forehead bent forward.

     Use high camera level.

     Use full frontal face view.

Receding Chin:

     Head tilted backward.

     Use low camera level.

     Use full frontal face view.

Double Chin:

     Tilt chin up.

     Use high camera level.

     Have subject lean forward slightly and project chin.

     Use full frontal face view.

Tense Jaw:

     Ask subject to wiggle jaw to loosen muscles.

Hollow Cheeks:

     Use high camera level.

     Tilt head backward.

     Use left or right partial face view.

Large Mouth:

     Head bent slightly forward.

     Use left or right partial face view.

Small Mouth:

Use left or right partial face view.

Mouth closed with jaw relaxed.

Use high camera level.

Slanted/Crooked Lipline:

Tilt subject's head so lipline is parallel to shoulder line.

Turn subject to partial view, the side of face with higher lipline is towards camera.

Avoid large smiles as they make crooked lipline more prominent.

Consider profile view.

Nose Pull:

Photograph into the pull.

Long Nose:

Tilt chin upward.

Use full frontal face view.

Use lower camera level.

Short Nose:

Lower the chin.

Use higher camera level.

Increase shadow under nose.

Angular Nose:

Use full frontal face view.

Crooked Nose:

Use left or right partial face view.

Photograph into the curve.

Broken Nose:

A broken nose often has a high and low side. Photograph into high side.

Neck Cord or Muscles:

Tilt head until cord disappears.

Lower head.

Large Roman Nose:

Use full frontal face view.

Use normal camera level.

Baldness:

Place top of head in shadow.

Blend top of head with background.

Use lower camera level.

Thinning Hair:

If on only one side, place this side away from camera. If thin all over, use low lighting on head.

Dark Hair:

Use high lighting.

Contrast color from background.

Light Hair:
    Use low lighting.
    Contrast color from background.
Heaviness:
    Blend clothes and background.
    Use short lighting.
    Use low contrast lighting.
Large Hips:
    Have subject put weight on back foot, turn hips away from
        camera and then turn shoulders back toward camera.

Selection of Clothes for a Portrait

Clothes Communicate with Color and Style

Clothes provide one of the first non-verbal impressions an individual communicates about himself as he dresses for himself and society. Whether the clothes originate for warmth, protection from the elements, modesty, utility, power, identity, vanity, sexual adornment, or magic to ward off evil spirits each item of clothing acts as a loudly or softly spoken word. Just like a person who won't say certain words, there is an individual who won't wear certain clothes.

Clothes consist of colors that direct the viewer's eye, emit emotions, and create moods and illusions. There is no right or wrong to color, only reactions to color.

Style developed throughout history and is influenced by world events. Dynasties of kings and pharaohs ruled the ancient world, which enabled a style to remain for hundreds of years. Any change in style came when power changed, because wealth ruled or a style created a reaction.

In the overall history of style, men dressed more elaborately than women. Men from the sixteenth century to the nineteenth century dressed in lace, satin, fur, and ribbons. This elaborate dressing reached its zenith in the reign of the French king, Louis XIV, who personally reigned from 1661 to 1715. Since the early 1800s, women's dress has overshadowed men's attire.

The unisex style in the latter half of the twentieth century represents the mid-swing of the pendulum between men's or women's elaborate dress. Both men and women began wearing naturally the unisex clothing such as blue jeans, trousers, and boots with a naturalness.

Designers create clothing styles that mirror our times. Clothes styles can be so advanced they look absurd and daring.

Or, clothes can be so behind their time that they appear charming, quaint, and romantically nostalgic. Clothes worn during the style's peak are considered smart.

Although modern-day times dictate a hurried pace and forced self-service, these situations evolve into a "clothes of the day" style of casualness and informality. The clothes of the day are presented in a portrait in a "dressed up" casualness with artistic expression to celebrate the ordinary.

Selection of Clothes Color Scheme by Percentages

The color of clothes selected for a person to wear in a portrait is governed first by the overall body color scheme of the person influenced by the color of skin, hair, eyes, and lips. Each person has a harmony of colors complimentary to him and each color projects a special effect. Skin is the subject's background color and is the first consideration in selecting a color.

After you have declared the mood of the overall portrait by using monochromatic, analogous, complimentary, or triadic color schemes as discussed in Selection of Portrait Color Scheme by Relationships on page 60-61, a selection of clothes color adds further harmony. The two schemes of selecting color—Selection of Portrait Color Scheme by Relationships and Selection of Clothes Color Scheme by Percentages—often overlap.

To establish an effective proportion of color, percentages or ratios are used. See Using Color for Portraiture on the back cover: Part V, Selection of Clothes Color Scheme by Percentages. Selection by percentages is merely proportioning the ratio of color to relate to the overall mood of the portrait such as monochromatic, analogous, complimentary, or triadic.

Selection of clothes color scheme by percentages involves:
• One-color scheme
• Two-color scheme
• Three-color scheme
• Multi-color scheme

These color schemes are used harmoniously with an analogous or complimentary arrangement in all these forms except the one-color scheme. Color is seldom isolated, but combined with other colors, if only in a background.

The one-color scheme is 100% of one color and small variations of the same color. It's almost impossible to put together perfect matches of one color because of different textures. Perfectly matched colors aren't as interesting to the eye as blending colors. Even in the one-color scheme, light to medium to dark shades portray subtle differences. Shades are graduated on the body from the darker shades at the bottom to the lightest shades at the top. See Using Color for Portraiture on the back cover: Part V, Selection of Clothes Color Scheme by Percentages.

A two color scheme is 70% to 90% of a major color mixed with 10%-30% of a minor color. A preferential combination is two colors which are complimentary (opposite on the color wheel) or analogous (adjacent on the color wheel). Select first the major color and then select the minor color. The eye is led first to the point where the two colors meet. Varying shades of one color in a two-color scheme are considered part of one color. See Using Color for Portraiture on the back cover: Part V, Selection of Clothes Color Scheme by Percentages.

A three color scheme is 70% of a major color, 20% of a minor color and 10% of a sub-minor color. A preferential combination is in analogous or complimentary form. The sub-minor color energizes and electrifies, is used more than once, and adds the forceful vitality because the viewer's eye travels first to the third color. An example: a small amount of color in a man's tie, a flower in a woman's hand, a belt at a woman's waist, or a pin on a dress. See Using Color for Portraiture on the back cover: Part V, Selection of Clothes Color Scheme by Percentages.

A multi-color scheme has more than three colors in varying percentages. The viewer's eye enjoys a multi-color scheme if the major color is one hue, preferably in the background occupying the most space in a plaid or floral design. If not, a multi-color scheme is discordant and confusing to the eye. See Using Color for Portraiture on the back cover: Part V, Selection of Clothes Color Scheme by Percentages.

Selection of Clothing Style for a Portrait

Clothing styles "date" a portrait because the portrait emerges from a period that fostered the clothing style. Dating is kept to a minimum by using clothes that reflect minimum extremes and don't relate to fads.

Style relates to the times. Some eras promote clothes that make a person look too mature, while other eras promote clothes that make the wearer look too juvenile. Clothes look best when worn for the right occasion and setting.

The region in which a person lives dictates the style. Some regions are more stylish, while others are more casual or ethnic.

Persons have definite reasons for wearing or not wearing certain style of clothes. If you prefer one style of clothes and the subject doesn't like that style, then you shouldn't ask the subject to wear the style not to his liking. The subject obviously associates the clothes style or color with an unpleasantness and this shows ill effects in the portrait. Usually a person wears what he thinks looks good.

Conversely, if the subject does not know what clothing style looks best on him, according to his times, status, or age, the subject depends on you to indicate what looks best in a portrait.

The proportions of the body are emphasized or subdued with clothing styles. The study of the body proportions as discussed on pages 93-99 aids in the clothes selection.

Clothing selection is not an exact science, but the following guidelines will help you.

Woman

The shape of the face as discussed on pages 93-99, Figures 7-1, 7-2, and 7-3 determines the neckline of the woman's clothes.

A woman subject with a round face looks best in an elongated neck line such as a V-neck, with vertical lines of jewelry in necklace and earrings.

A woman subject with an elongated face looks best with horizontal lines to broaden the face.

A woman subject with a square face looks best with the square softened by using round lines of design such as an oval shaped neckline with slightly curved jewelry.

The V-necklines are crisp, clear, and uncomplicated. A V-neck line, in most instances, is the preferred neckline with the jewelry adding to the lines of design. The V-neck makes the neck appear long and elegant and provides the head with a long, united pedestal base.

The second preferred neckline choice is a neckline giving elongation to the neck such as square, boat neck, scallop, or off-the-shoulders. These styles reveal collarbones and shoulder bones and if these areas are unattractive avoid them in a portrait. A turtleneck foreshortens the neck.

Long sleeves are preferred, whether in a blouse, shirt, coat, jacket, or sweater, to avoid a long expanse of bare arm. Short sleeves are worn only for a special purpose. A young woman wears short sleeves more easily than an older woman.

A solid color in a medium tone is an excellent choice in clothes. Very bright colors for anyone over thirty years of age offend the viewer's eye. Avoid prints, florals, stripes, and plaids because they detract and "date" easily.

If using a solid color or pattern is unavoidable, dominance

offers a good guide. When the person wearing the clothes enters the room, if the clothes are noticed first, the pattern is too busy, or the color too bold. The first preference is to see the person first and the clothes second.

Patterns have more weight than solid colors and appear heavier in the lines of design. If the subject insists on a pattern, then do your best in photographing her.

Dresses, rather than separate pieces in different colors, add height to a short woman.

Jackets that dip slightly at the back of the neck add length to a short neck.

Shirt pockets add clutter and weight to the subject. Wide jacket lapels add width to the subject.

Shoes contribute to the overall line of design. Darker shoes act as a base and give stability. If the subject is heavier in the hip line, the darker shoes help disguise the large hips.

Keep shoes the same color as the dress hemline, or darker, especially if the hemline is navy, black, or brown. Slacks provide an exception because the legs appear in an unbroken color line.

Dyed-to-match shoes present a dramatic coordinated look.

Silver shoes look good with cool colors. Gold shoes look good with warm colors.

Ankle shoe straps on a short legged woman shorten the length of the leg.

Sleek feminine pumps or boots that aren't form fitting are best for a woman with thick legs. Avoid heavy looking shoes or boots.

Plump feet look best in shoes with tapered toes or a V-throat. Skinny legs and feet look best in round or oval toed shoes. Any type of asymmetrical shoe creates a longer looking leg.

In hosiery, sheer, transparent hosiery looks lighter and thinner than opaque hosiery. A gray-beige color offers the most versatile, time-tested color. Fun colors, such as white and pastels, blend well when matched with the shoe color and look best when coordinated with similar upper body color.

Fur pieces have their own colors and personalities. For example: mink and sable are sophisticated, fox is independent, and bulky rabbit is fun.

A preferred handbag prop is a small, clutch purse. Handbags are in the same mood as the dress—sporty, casual, dressy, or after-five. The traditional approach blends or matches the handbag with shoes; but handbags can be a color taken from the undertone of the clothes.

Belts represent the ten percent third color that the viewer's eye sees. Some better dresses don't come with belts because women consider the belt an accessory that is individualized. Lines of design are extended or shortened by belts. A short-waisted subject needs a narrow belt. A wide belt disguises part of the hipline.

Jewelry, as a personal expression, becomes part of the 10% third color, especially if red, jade, or coral. Shiny surfaces such as metal, glass, semi-precious, and precious stones reflect light.

Gold jewelry looks good with warm colors. White gold, platinum, ivory, and pearl jewelry look good with cool colors. Diamonds, in any jewelry, reflect light, which makes them effective. The old saying applies, "Don't wear diamonds in the daytime unless you have them."

Necklaces add to the total effect giving a definite horizontal or vertical line to the neckline. A choker shortens the neck and covers up an aging throat. For a woman with a large bosom a good necklace length is between the chin and bosom. Each time a woman turns her body in a pose the necklace should be adjusted, if necessary.

Pins result in a white spot if light hits them wrong. Tilt pin away from light to avoid glare.

Earrings contribute to a finished look, add to the subject's beauty, and compliment the facial structure line by not being noticed first.

When selecting earrings for the clothes, maintain the degree of formality such as faddish, traditional, dressy, or sporty.

The selection of earrings depends more on the shape of the face than the clothes or color of the earring. Study the face and notice the contour line from the chin to top of the head.

Earrings create an illusion and accent the best features. If the subject's eyes are beautiful, earrings are selected to lead the viewer's eye to the subject's eyes. If the subject's mouth looks interesting, earrings are selected to lead the viewer's eye to the mouth.

An earring shape counterbalances the facial shape. The oval face accepts most earring shapes and is scaled to the face and body. The round face looks best in vertical lines such as oval or marquis shaped earrings. The right earring for a square face is longer than they are wide. The narrow face looks good is any shape adding width with horizontal lines leading the viewer's eye from one side to another side.

Consider the length of the neck. If the subject's neck is short, don't use long earrings because they pull the head closer to the shoulder. A dangling earring draws attention to the jowl or wrinkled neck skin. The motion of a swinging, dangling earring with a slow shutter speed causes a blur.

The color of an earring relates to the eye color and hair rather than the color of the clothes. Blue eyes look good with sapphire, blue topaz, lapis, and aquamarine earrings. Green eyes look good with gold, emerald, coral, jade, and ruby earrings. Brown eyes look good with emerald, topaz, and pearl earrings. Black earrings worn with brown eyes make the eyes recede unless the black is trimmed in gold or diamonds.

Skin color dictates the use of the metal color. Olive skin looks good with silver, platinum, and white gold. Gold skin looks good with gold, bronze, and copper. Everyone looks good with yellow gold. A gray haired woman avoids wearing silver or platinum earrings.

To lighten a subject's eyes, use a darker color earring than the eye. To darken the subject's eyes, use a lighter color earring than the eyes.

Perfume, an accessory that doesn't show, lends an accompaniment to the overall atmosphere. Whether morning or late afternoon, the subject wants to wear her favorite.

Make-up acts like an expression because it conveys a message. Make-up creates an illusion that the face conforms to an ideal in time and space.

Make-up adds or detracts from the portrait, according to how applied. Women subjects, by their choice, vary in make-up application from a perfectly made-up face to a face with no make-up. Neither is right or wrong, but what the woman considers best for herself.

Make-up offers another situation where you assess the situation. A face with heavy make-up looks artificial and aging. Facial flaws may photograph harshly with no make-up. You can offer general suggestions, such as: don't overdo make-up because the camera exaggerates, or lightly contouring the face with subtle make-up enhances the portrait because the camera flattens features.

The best make-up base is medium tone and light weight in feeling. The eyebrows are brushed up. Eye make-up makes eyes the center of attention. A softened black, brown, or navy eyeliner is appropriate. A too heavily lined eye looks smaller and squinty. Use eyeliner on the bottom of the eye only three-fourths of the way in from the outer corner to open the eye. Use cream eye shadow on the upper lid in tones of brown, gray, taupe, and green. Avoid blue and frosted eye shadow. Apply mascara heavily on the top eyelashes and normally or lightly on the bottom eyelashes. Keep the rouge or blush line high on the cheekbone. Avoid the rouge or blush line near the ear, nose, or eye. Lipstick should be a medium hue that avoids blue or brown undertones. Avoid frosted lipsticks.

Powder, if any, should be light and used sparingly on the forehead, nose, and chin. Too much powder causes the skin to look older and drier. A shine on the face is preferable to a dry, older look.

Hair represents a woman's crowning glory and carries an aura that permeates the subject and the viewer. The hair extends past the head, surrounds the woman and is similar to putting a parenthesis after the individual's name such as gentle, chic, or sporty.

Hair looks best when shiny and luxurious because hair catches light with its sheen.

The degree of femininity is shown by the hair and relates to the person's age. Younger women usually wear their hair longer and dangling loose to give an informal look. Hair worn loosely is used to shape a broad face by moving the hair forward to thin the face. Upswept hair exposes prominent ears and is avoided by posing the face in a partial view. Older women wear their hair in a shorter, set style. Light and gray hair is lighted in lower light levels to give the hair a softer look with more detail.

A woman spends as much time on her hair as the clothes selection. Moderation applies to hair styles, because hair conveys a message.

Man

In selecting a man's clothes for a portrait, the traditional attire of coat and tie simplifies the selection, yet limits the selection. When the classic portrait is made with more casual attire, the clothes selection broadens.

To give the head a stable base a coat and tie create an illusion of the V-neck, while the open collar, jacket, or sweater are actually a V-neck.

In selecting a classic, traditional suit, the basic colors seldom change and "date." A man can't tolerate as much color in a portrait as a woman.

The first preference of suit colors include charcoal, gray, navy, black, or brown. Dark-toned suits carry more authority. Brown suits appear more country than urban.

Choices are dictated by geographical customs. Those who live in the northern and eastern United States favor dark and conservative suits. Those in the south and western United States wear not only dark and conservative suits, but light and sporty suits. Sometimes it's impossible to avoid regionalism.

A first choice in suits is a year-round fabric in a solid color. A subtle pattern or plaid is acceptable.

The first choice of shirt color is white. Sand, taupe, light gray, light blue, and light yellow are acceptable, but they date a portrait. A patterned shirt, such as a slight stripe, is an acceptable choice if the stripes are maintained straight. Dark shirts are worn only without a tie with very casual attire such as slacks and blue jeans. Using dark shirts and ties with suits can date a portrait.

The shirt is long sleeved, even in summertime. If the long-sleeved shirt is worn with a coat and tie, the cuff of the shirt shows about 1/4" to 1/2" past the sleeve cuff of the coat. If the long-sleeved shirt is worn with an open collar, without a coat, the sleeve cuff is buttoned or rolled up slightly for a casual look.

If the man has a tattoo on his forearm, suggest that he roll the sleeve down and button the cuff to avoid a large expanse of bare arm.

Any words on the shirt are only the man's monogram.

The tie accents the suit by coordinating with a color from the suit. The tie pattern size is important because the smaller the pattern, the less it dates. The narrow stripped tie and the narrower repeated stripe indicate order and conservativeness in the fabric. A diagonally striped tie is acceptable with a striped shirt. If the pattern of the shirt and suit slightly conflict, the tie links it together.

Ties agree with the suit in mood and texture such as dressy, business-like, or sporty.

An ascot is worn in place of a tie to create an illusion of a V-neck and blends with the shirt and suit.

The choice of shoes is dark brown or black. Darker shoes look better with a light-colored suit. Hosiery matches the shoes.

The first choice in clothes selection for the classic man's portrait is a solid colored suit, solid white shirt, and patterned tie. The second choice is a subtly patterned suit, solid white shirt, and patterned or solid tie.

Child

In clothes selection regarding the shape of the face, the same rules apply for a child as a man and woman.

Simplicity marks the key to children's clothing because you don't want anything to detract from a child's outstanding qualities, such as youthful beauty, spontaneity, and purity of facial and body expressions.

In small children, short sleeves look better because the long expanse of a youthful looking arm doesn't detract. The first preference for small children is clear, primary colors rather than muddy-colored clothes. Toddler boys look best in round Peter Pan collars or no collar.

Groups

Clothing for a group should coordinate around one chosen individual.

The "chosen member" in a family group is the mother. Parents are put in darker clothes so they don't overpower the children.

In a group of children, the oldest child is the chosen member because sibling rivalry commands attention.

In a group of businessmen, the chosen member is the Chairman of the Board, Chief Executive Officer, or President.

⁓ E I G H T ⁓

HARMONIOUS INTEGRITY

Defining Harmonious Integrity

Harmonious integrity is your ability to assemble all the building blocks for the construction of a portrait with rhythm and balance resulting in a trusted blending known as "your style."

Harmonious integrity, an elusive element, resides in everyone. Nothing or no one can take harmonious integrity from you, nor do you ever lose harmonious integrity.

The building blocks that you've learned from studying this handbook, used as guidelines, and broken when there is a reason, allow you to approach your subject in an uninhibited and independent manner. This independence gives you the ability to produce compositions that have movement and unity to create harmonious integrity.

Harmonious integrity exists in your conscious or subconscious. However, if concepts don't surface, there isn't a need for creative efforts.

Ultimately, harmonious integrity invokes in the viewer a sense of pleasure from viewing blended, well-organized elements.

Origins of Harmonious Integrity

The well-organized, blended, and presented building blocks result from gaining knowledge by reasoning, intuition, experiencing the senses, and from authorities. In chapter two, Your Enrichment, reasoning, intuition, and experiencing the senses were discussed.

In order to develop harmonious integrity you, the student,

gather knowledge from different types of teachers serving as authorities. All teachers have credentials and a good teacher has the respect of other teachers. The best teachers are constantly learning because teaching is one of the best ways to learn.

Teachers are categorized in several different ways:

• One type leads in a traditional approach where students idolize and copy the masters.

• Another type leads in the non-traditional approach and encourages you to ignore the masters and move in different paths. The goal is to break the rules at any cost.

• Another type combines, favorably, the best of the traditional and non-traditional approaches.

Regardless of the direction the teacher guides you, there is a natural tendency to follow the approach of your first teacher.

You should find an approach that's comfortable, yet one that frees you from the fear of "stepping out" to new adventures.

The best teacher isn't always the most knowledgeable or efficient but one who inspires you to reach for your full potential by stimulating your desire for more knowledge.

The best teacher provides a good mental atmosphere by not being too critical or too lenient. But, the teacher should guide you to what is "best for you." Peers are also useful to give feedback on your work, but remember that their critiques represent only an opinion.

The best teacher creates an atmosphere that contains enough positive tension between discipline and disorder to create an energy flow.

The best teacher also provides visual demonstration and verbal instruction in an atmosphere that triggers a dialogue between the teacher and you. This environment encourages creativity in a proper mental and physical space and provides the time, privacy, and solitude to develop this mental activity to the hilt.

The best teacher is usually the best by being a good role model. The quality of the teacher relates directly to the teacher's personal inner quality.

The best teacher teaches you everything he knows, encourages you to stay with him until you know all that he knows, and then encourages you branch out to your own style.

The best teacher allows you freedom of choice which is essential to growth.

Teaching is an act of generous giving. Learning is the joyful acceptance of that generous gift.

Growth of Harmonious Integrity

To reach the maximum of your potential it's essential to experience personal and historical growth in addition to technical and cultural growth.

To achieve artistic growth, you grow personally on a day-to-day basis, which can't be taught in a classroom. You should be actively involved with all five senses in the business of living. These experiences enhance your perception. Then you discover your soul is full. Now you create to empty the soul which then requires refilling. Creativity is always the need to express this internal content.

You also grow by studying the history of photography. The early comparison of black and white photographs was to the available art forms. Study everything—the masters of oil portraiture, drawings, and sculpture. Remember, history is the breeding ground where collective energy is stored and absorbed to become the catalyst for the creative process.

And you should grow technically which can be taught. Learn your craft. If there is something to communicate and it is poorly presented with inferior technical quality, the communication is lost.

You must grow culturally, which can't be taught, but develops in the course of interaction, circumstances, and instances in day-to-day living.

If your portraiture only expresses your personal and cultural references, your work will show little dimension. If your portraiture is produced with only history and technical reference, the work is unoriginal and is boring to the viewer. Yet, in the development of all four areas, you change, and your own style will emerge.

MY PERSONAL PARTICIPATION

Here's how I incorporated all the building blocks I've talked about in this handbook into my preferred procedures. This is only how I work, so take what you want.

The making of a classic outdoor color portrait begins with the first meeting between the potential client and myself.

The client I accept must be appropriate for my technique, intelligent use of photographic history, personal tastes, and cultural aspects of my life, which are blended into a harmonious whole that is unique to me and called "my style."

I firmly establish myself as the director and use the appropriate building blocks with precision. The success ration is more assured if I develop an advance plan. This planning is time consuming—the actual making of the portrait takes only a fraction of a second—but is rewarding. The portrait work ends for me when I present the portrait to the client.

The most challenging assignments are those with clients about whom I know nothing. In these cases, I search for more information. I never know my capacity until I'm tested in this way.

I reinforce this challenge by reminding myself that portraiture offers an interaction with people on a one-to-one basis. I have a innate interest and curiosity about people and the portrait is the way I express that interest. A fine portrait is not made accidentally but by the devotion of my mind, eye, and heart. I am then a participant as well as spectator.

As a portraitist, I am fortunate to be a woman. Even though women, for a long time, weren't entitled or didn't allow themselves to engage in activities that society declared as "man's territory," I have, as a woman, access to a private mental world that a man can only guess about.

And seeing through a woman's eye, I can take the male viewer into a world that has been unexplored by him. Man doesn't at first understand through a woman's eye, but today he pretends to comprehend, which ultimately leads to understanding. The woman's eye for sensitivities challenges the man to go beyond his past concepts and explore a broader concept.

Since women, men, children, and families are all my subject matter, I photograph them through the vision that I bring from my world as a woman. I avoid the sentimentality, that can easily develop, by using my craft.

In portraiture, I resist the pressures of the outside world, to avoid the historic and never-ending homemaker role as a substitute for creativity. I want to balance my love of work, photography, and self-discipline. From man's world, I take the technical skill and authority. From the woman's world, I bring my vision and intuition. The key is to co-ordinate all these factors.

Portraiture, whether created through a man's or woman's eye, is a challenge. If I don't rise to this challenge, my creative life is empty. From this struggle comes the "best" portrait.

If I photograph "from without" to record and document, I usually decide whether to report the subject "as is" or use my creativity. If I photograph creatively, I have no choice but to express "from within."

But there is a fine line between expressing what I see or want to see and the commercialism of what I am paid to see. I handle this situation by inquiring what ideas my client has about the portrait. This allows the client to be a participant in the creative process.

Most people have a preconceived idea about what they want or think they want, in the portrait, but don't know how to explain themselves, so there are few ideas with which to work.

If my client doesn't have any ideas of what he wants, I present my portfolio, which is carefully bound in a standard size album. This shows the care and concern involved in my portrait work, and they usually respect my creativity. My responsibility is not just the "proper aperture exposure," but the proper presentation.

I also present in advance a price list for each type of finish, any enhancing work, size of portrait, and duplicate copies. I also include a "creative session" fee based on the number of persons photographed. (The creative session fee is collected when the portrait is made. A deposit is required when the order is placed.)

Part of the creative session fee is a clothes conference. Most clients are pleased to have this service especially if I give easy, clear choices. A clothes conference shows I care, heightens my client's expectations, furthers my acquaintance with the client, and builds confidence.

If the client agrees to the clothing conference, I arrange an appointment at his home. At the conference, I expand the meeting into a pre-visualization session. My "eye" is now the camera, but I add dimensions by taking my camera and light meter along to possibly find a home location and visually compose the portrait. If I'm unable to take the camera I take a 2 1/4 x 2 1/4 empty black cardboard slide mount format to simulate the camera format.

While at the client's home, I look for a good location which depends on the number of people to be in the portrait and the degree of formality or casualness required by the client. A formal portrait requires a location with preferred vertical lines. A casual portrait requires a location with preferred horizontal lines.

Outdoor portrait locations can be a small area anywhere, everywhere, and under every condition. I look for lines of design rather than situations where a yard is raked or mowed, for unlikely places such as a corner in a yard, or an overhanging tree branch.

In deciding on the location I first consider the lighting, then foreground and background. In my pre-visualization I pose the subject with the clothing selection with the props in the lighting, foreground, and background. This "thinking through" is essential to control all tonal values so attention is directed to the subject's face.

I enjoy making portraits at the subject's home because I don't have to transport the subject mentally or physically to unfamiliar surroundings. And this is comforting to the subject because he feels at home, literally, and this gives me insight into the subject's life style and environment. The client's home is a new viewpoint and inspires me. Making the portrait at home also makes it easier for the subject to change clothes. Home also provides many props that I can use if appropriate.

I live in a heavily-forested area, so if I don't use the subject's home, I find a location that is at the edge of the forest, which provides more light than in mid-forest. Mid-forest lighting filters down through the trees to form down-lighting which ages any face.

I then consider the working space I will have for my equipment and the subject. I like the subject to stand 6 to 8 feet from the background. I make a final decision on the location after leaving the clothing conference and pre-visualization session.

At the clothing conference, without his knowledge, I analyze my subject's face, body, and skin color. The darker the skin color, the more noticeable the light on the skin. I note special features that need enhancing such as drooping shoulders, thick hips, heavy ankles, and bald heads. I note the features to emphasize such as graceful hands, long waists, and red hair.

A clothing conference may appear unnecessary at first but I prefer advance "arranged choices" rather than having to deal on location with a subject's possible shocking and surprising clothes selection.

If I don't like the client's clothes selection such as romantic, sporty, gamin, dramatic or ingenue, I tactfully suggest the subject make two selections. If one doesn't photograph well, there is an alternate selection. However, working with two selections is time-consuming at the actual creative session and tiresome for the client and me.

If permitted, I actually look in the client's closet and select the one or two selections. I look at the clothes in natural lighting instead of artificial lighting, particularly fluorescent, which distorts colors. I then lay out the clothes in the client's home and arrange possibilities for the portrait. I keep the choices to a minimum to avoid giving the client too many decisions.

If the portrait is a family group I begin the clothes selection with the mother. Man has latitude in his appearance, a child looks appealing in almost anything, but a woman has less latitude in her appearance.

I begin each clothing conference as if arranging paint on an artist's palette. I decide how many colors to work with and how they blend with any possible background. See Using Color for Portraiture on the back cover: Part IV, Selection of Portrait Color Scheme by Relationships, and Part V, Selection of Clothes Color Scheme by Percentages. The grouping of colors has endless possibilities.

In general cool colors enhance skin tones. Carefully consider and beware of yellow, pink, red, and orange because they often compete with skin tones.

Other considerations influence the clothes selection:

• Ask where the finished portrait is to be placed because it makes a difference in the vertical or horizontal composition if the portrait is to be placed on a desk, or hung on a wall in a den, office, or living room.

• Ask what size the finished portrait is to be because if small, the image of the face needs to be as large as possible.

• Ask additional questions that may come up as a result of the clothing conference regarding the number of persons in the portrait: how many are adults and children; if children, their ages.

• Ask if the client wants more than one portrait. If two

portraits are placed together for example, it creates a pleasing effect to have the subjects in the portraits facing each other and dressed compatibly.

• Ask about any interests of the person or group for possible props. To have props engages the viewer's eye and tells a story.

• Don't ask about including a pet, but if the client mentions a pet, agree to include the pet, but point out the difficulties. The disadvantage for me is that paying so much attention to an animal I can miss something with the subjects. If the client insists, be sure the animal is groomed, has relieved itself before the session, and allowed to roam before posing. Place the animal in the portrait according to his size and color. Position the animal last on the edge of the group or in an open space. Dogs are positioned sitting or lying down. If the dog's attention can be focused on toys, food, or noises, its ears perk up and this adds alertness. Also, assure the owner that the animal is behaving quite normally, no matter what. The essential ingredients in including an animal in a portrait are patience, take lots of film, and make many exposures.

With all this information I visually compose where each subject sits or stands. This gives further control over clothes selection; for example, who wears a dark shirt, dress, or slacks. Avoid having all the dark colors in the upper portion of the portrait as in shirts, blouses, or sweaters. Conversely, all dark in the portrait should not be placed in the lower portion such as slacks, jeans, trousers, or skirts. Mix the dark and light colors for vertical and horizontal separation.

While at the clothing conference I may make the following suggestions:

• For the woman, I suggest that she make her portrait appointment soon after her appointment with her hairdresser or whenever she coiffures her hair. But the best time for the portrait is not immediately after her hair is coiffured at a beauty salon because of the possible harsh look. A good suggestion is that she not try a new hairdo.

• Suggest to the woman who wears dramatic make-up to start the session with lighter-applied make-up and graduate to heavier-applied make-up because dramatic make-up can overpower the portrait. In this way, the woman has a choice.

• Suggest to the woman to consider the shape of her jewelry because it gives shape to the face.

• Suggest that the older woman use a refining mask several hours before the portrait. This refreshes tired skin, tightens the skin, and generally uplifts the spirit.

• Suggest that the man or boy have his hair cut a few days

before the portrait to avoid a shorn appearance.

• Inquire if anyone wears glasses and suggest that the glasses be checked for alignment. Consider asking that tinted lenses not be worn because they hide the eyes, date the portrait, and make a shadow. Ask if the frames are dark and large, because they cast a shadow on the eyes.

• Suggest, according to the season, that everyone avoid any situation that could result in a sunburn.

• After the clothes and accessories are determined, suggest that the client telephone you if any clothes selection is changed. If a client changes the clothes selection and fails to notify me, then I do the best with the changed choice. If a second change of clothes is planned, then after several exposures in the first selection, suggest the client change to the second selection.

I prime myself by looking at other portraitists' work and my own previous portraits to tap into my potential before I decide on the final composition. I subscribe to the better photography magazines, which aren't always the most popular, and clip portraits that I feel are useful. I keep a notebook with other portraitists' work of poses, locations, and ideas for easy reference.

If, I have a "photographer's block," which is only a matter of "what do I do next," I communicate with other art forms such as reading a biography, listening to music, studying a painting, or even reading a children's book. Inspiration comes from unlikely sources. Also, I try to look at the situation from a different perspective by taking the assignment apart and change my creative order. If this doesn't inspire me, I make a portrait because the actual process of making a portrait often inspires me.

Sometimes my portraits develop a mind of their own that I must control by placing my "pre-visualized" portrait on a "blueprint." I make this preliminary sketch mentally or on paper so the subject won't have to pose a long time. Granted, a planned portrait could lose its spontaneity, but the portrait gains in the control of poses, expressions, and attitudes of both the subject and myself.

I set the exact day for the portrait by selecting two or three possible days that the portrait can be made. I always photograph on the first chosen day because if the weather is uncooperative, I have one or two more days to make the portrait.

For adults, I prefer making a portrait around 3:00 P.M. The exact time can vary an hour, depending on the lighting conditions and the seasonal sun's angle. My second choice is around 10:00 A. M. For small children I arrange the time of day that is best for them. For infants the best time is after a nap or meal.

Preparing for an assignment includes checking that my equipment is clean, in working order, simple, and available. For each outdoor assignment, my equipment is basically the same with a few additions or deletions. I never experiment with new equipment while at a creative session.

My list of equipment:
- Hasselblad Aluminum Carrying Case, 18" x 14" x 6," with name and address for identification. The case is sturdy enough to stand on.
- Hasselblad 500 C/M Camera Body
- Carl Zeiss Sonnar CF f/4 150mm Lens
- Carl Zeiss Distagon CF f/3.5 60mm Lens
- Hasselblad Warming Filter 50 1 x CR3 -O for 150mm Lens
- Nikon Soft Focus Filter No. 1, 52mm, used with Lens Thread Adapter for 150mm Lens
- Hasselblad Polarizing Filter/63 2 x Pola -1 for 60mm Lens
- Hasselblad Polarizing Filter/50 2 x Pola - for 150mm Lens
- Hasselblad Lens Shade for focal lengths from 100 to 250 mm
- Two Hasselblad A12 Film Magazines for 12 2 1/4 x 2 1/4 frames each on 120 roll film
- Hasselblad Prism Viewfinder NC-2/100 which yields an unreversed image three times larger than focusing screen image
- Hasselblad Focusing Screen with central grid
- Remote Control Cord
- Honeywell Pentax Exposure Meter, 1deg/21deg, with strap
- Vivitar Electronic Flash 102
- Vivitar Automatic Electronic Flash Model 283
- Hasselblad Attachment for electronic strobe
- Two Connecting cords
- Vivitar Remote Flash Trigger SL-2
- Liquid Lens cleaner to put on Kodak Lens Cleaning Paper
- Kodak Lens Cleaning Paper
- Extra AA and 9V Batteries
- Dust-off
- A Twelve Foot Measuring String
- 120 Roll Film—if the weather is extremely hot, I carry the film separately in a small ice chest with Ice Gel.

In an elongated traveling bag, I carry:
- 1 Larson Enterprises, Inc. Silver Reflectasol-Hex Umbrella
- 1 Larson Enterprises, Inc. Gold Reflectasol-Hex Umbrella
- 1 Tripod with a string holding the three legs together
- 1 Stand with Accessory Arm

- A Set of Leg Weights
- A Black Head Screen and Stand

I carry an assortment of "first aid" items in my camera bag:
- Masking Tape
- Safety Pins
- Straight Pins
- Clothes Pins
- Hand Towel to wipe off seats or benches
- Mirror
- Comb
- Astringent Lotion with cotton balls to freshen the subject's face when the weather is hot
- Light and Dark Towels to sit on while the subject is posing
- Large Garbage Bags to protect camera equipment in case of rain
- Rubber bands
- Q-Tips
- Small Screwdriver
- Instruction Manuals for camera equipment
- Insect Spray
- Bug Repellent
- Folding Ladder to allow me to raise tripod to its full extension

If you're just starting your portraiture activities, I suggest you use only one camera format until good results are established. This allows consistency as you learn.

A good portrait lens is the large format camera but with the convenience of roll film and film technology the differences between film size and film quality is reduced to permit the use of a smaller format camera.

I use a Hasselblad 500 C/M camera which is a medium format with a square 2 1/4 x 2 1/4 negative. The square is static in horizontal or vertical movement. To create movement, I compose closely on assignment, and again in the darkroom if necessary.

The three basic lenses are normal, wide angle, and telephoto. The normal lens views approximately the same way the human eye views. The wide angle lens views more than the normal lens to make the subject smaller and increases the depth of field. The wide angle lens exaggerates anything close to the camera. The telephoto lens views the scene smaller than the normal lens to make the subject appear larger and closer, compresses the depth of field, and flattens perspective and therefore, does not enhance facial features. Additionally, you have to stand too far from the subject.

Within the normal lens range most portraitists use a lens about l 1/2 to 3 times the normal focal length. The portrait lens for a 35mm camera is from 85mm to 135mm. I prefer 135mm. The portrait lens for a 2 1/4 x 2 1/4 camera is from 150mm to 180mm. I prefer 150mm. The portrait lens for a 4 x 5 camera is from 180mm to 225mm. The portrait lens for a 5 x 7 format is from 225mm to 350mm.

When you increase the subject-to-camera distance, perspective improves, and creates more of a distance between you and the subject, which relaxes your subject. Also with the increased subject-to-camera distance added to a decreased depth of field a more three dimensional roundness is achieved.

I use the 150mm portrait lens, which is a medium telephoto lens. The depth of field, the area in sharp focus from the foreground to background, is shallow, but not limiting and allows for a sharply focused subject with a blurred background and foreground. The more depth of field, the farther away you get from the subject without being too far. The distance from camera to subject is not intimidating. However, in portraiture, increasing the camera-to-subject distance flattens features on the face regardless of the lens. The narrower view with the portrait lens indicates less background to create a tighter portrait. If you use a normal lens for portraits, remember that what is closest to the camera appears larger such as hands, feet, nose, and knees. Partial and full length poses are less distorted.

The 150mm lens also compresses near-to-far subjects allowing the subject to appear closer to the background and gives the best image with the least distortion. The 150mm lens gives the best representation of the contours and gradations of the facial planes. All parts of the body are basically at the same distance from the camera, thus the subject is proportioned with little distortion. The lens is short and easily managed on location.

Depth of field varies with the size of the lens opening, the distance from camera to the subject, and the focal length of the lens. Depth of field becomes greater when the size of the lens opening decreases, the subject distance increases, and the focal length of the lens decreases while the subject distance is unchanged. Within the depth of field range place the subject about 1/3 into the range leaving about 2/3 in back of the subject.

Because the 150mm portrait lens has a narrow depth of field, and focus is critical, there are instances when I use the wide angle lens. Using the wide angle lens allows for a greater depth of field and includes important compositional background. By including more background, the subject appears smaller. Place the subject in the center or near the center to avoid distortion. If I use a wide angle lens and the sun is at a low angle, my shadow may be in the portrait.

I use a medium size lens shade because a large lens shade with bellows can be blown by any breeze. Any unwanted light such as flare is kept off the lens with a lens shade.

I use a remote control cord which prevents camera vibration, allows me maneuverability, and provides eye contact with the subject. If dealing with a nervous subject or restless child, I hold the remote control cord behind my back without the subject being aware. If doing a profile the use of a remote control cord makes eye contact possible.

I don't use a motor driven camera because the same pose is too easily repeated.

I use the 45 degree prism viewfinder in a magnified, unreversed image. I focus on the eye closest to the camera.

I use a filter to protect the lens. In the especially green environment of grass, bushes, and trees, I use a Hasselblad W-3 warming filter to warm skin tones from any green reflection.

A polarizing filter cancels reflections and glare from a shiny surface and enriches colors. The filter rotates 360 degrees in its mount and is adjusted by turning the outer ring. The amount of reflection reduced depends on the camera's angle (about 35 degrees) to the reflective surface. Reflected light in the atmosphere can be lessened when the camera lens is at a right angle (90 degrees) to the sun.

In side lighting, using a polarizing filter makes more separation between clouds and sky. There are times when I use a polarizing filter on sunny days to create a deeper blue sky, intensify color, and reduce glare.

A soft focus filter is a combination of diffusion and sharpness and breaks up the highlights by bleeding them into shaded areas. An unsharp or blurry portrait is not a soft focus portrait. A soft focus filter gives controlled softening of the extra sharp edges. The image is softest when the lens aperture is wide open and increases in sharpness as the lens opening is reduced. The soft focus filter is sharpest at the actual focus point. Focus with a small aperture, then reset the lens to the proper aperture. Avoid high contrast areas because the soft focus filter has a tendency to produce a halo of light around high contrast points.

If I use a softening filter, I use the Nikon No. 1. A homemade diffusing material is a piece of black French tulle fabric.

I particularly like to use the soft focus filter on a mature woman. Her age doesn't blot out her beauty, but the softening of the wrinkles adds a poetic look to the evidence of the quality of the woman's life.

I use a tripod with one tripod leg in front closest to the subject, and the two remaining tripod legs closest to me standing behind the camera, Figure 9-1.

This tripod position keeps me from stumbling over a tripod leg. Don't extend the tripod center post too high because vibration can occur. The tripod handles are convenient hooks for hanging light meter and other equipment.

My tripod allows loading and unloading of film without removing the camera from the tripod.

The camera mounted on a tripod facilitates the camera level from high to low and enables you to tilt the camera in all directions. The flexibility gained allows for variable shutter speeds, larger lens openings, and sharper focus.

If the lighting creates light spots on the subject, I use a small black head screen mounted with an accessory arm on an easy-to-move stand. The size of the black head screen is important to cover the offending light spots. Additional uses are for subduing gray hair, prominent ears, bald heads, and thinning and receding hairlines.

As a general rule, the camera height is where the film plane is parallel to the facial plane. In the head and shoulders pose, if the face is titled up or down for any Enhancing Techniques, as discussed on pages 127-132, the film plane should remain parallel to the face. In partial or full length poses, the film plane remains parallel with the body pose.

Camera height affects the facial, head, and torso expression and influences the mood of the portrait. As a result of studying the facial, head, and torso expressions, you may need to apply the Enhancing Techniques as listed on pages 127-132.

At head and shoulders position, the camera level is between the tip of the nose and the lips. At a partial position, the camera is level with the upper chest. At a full length position, the camera is at waist level or slightly below. A low camera level creates a sense of casualness. A high camera level tends to be more formal.

In photographing a child, place the camera at his level. In portraiture involving a child and adult, compromise by placing the camera level at a lower level.

On location I work with ambient lighting. I use a Pentax Spotmeter which enables me to take a close-up light meter reading from a distance. I position the facial pose at the appropriate angle and then read the shadow side of the face with the Spotmeter. If I

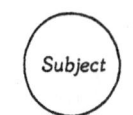

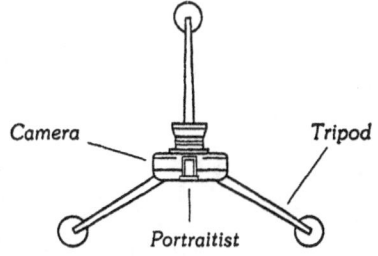

Figure 9-1
Tripod Position

stand close to the subject to take the reading, I wear medium tone clothes and stand to the side of the subject so I won't block any light. During an hour session, the light stays about the same, so I take only one light meter reading per pose if I stay within the basic location.

A gray card is a section of a gray-colored cardboard that reflects 18 percent of the light it receives, represents a medium tone, and is used when making exposure readings. I take the light meter reading and open up one stop because skin is darker than a gray card. For example, if my Spotmeter reads f/8, I open up to f/5.6. An incorrect exposure discolors skin tones. The exposure can be 2 stops over or ½ stop under and still produce a negative that is printable.

I photograph mostly at shutter speeds of 1/30 and 1/60 in the f/5.6 aperture range. As a portraitist I have no need for a fast shutter speed unless I am striving for a special effect.

The focus area of concern is from the eyebrow to chin which includes the eyes, nose, and mouth with the ears not necessarily in sharp focus. If some things are in soft focus the viewer's eye will settle first on what is in focus, which is the face.

A good guideline is:
• Use f/16, f/22, f/32 for pictorial photographs
• Use f/8 for subject matter not specific
• Use f/5.6, f/4, and f/2.8 for portraits and/or single theme

If I use a camera with a through-the-lens metering system or reflected meter readings, I stand near the subject, take the reading, set the camera, move back to the desired camera position, and make the exposure.

I personally don't care for any vignetting done with equipment as discussed on page 89. I create natural vignetting with the lines of design of the foreground and background. I don't want vignetting to be noticeable.

I prefer natural light for portraits, using side or back lighting. However, I can enhance natural lighting with additive or subtractive lighting as discussed on pages 76-77. In my part of the country, the light is on the minimum side, so I hesitate to use subtractive lighting in a true form. I add additive lighting by placing my subject so the light falls in the best places.

If I want to add artificial lighting as accent lighting, I use an electronic strobe in one of two ways:
• I mount the electronic strobe on top of the camera. Be sure the camera is aimed correctly at the subject so the light fall-off will not be offensive and noticeable. Power varies on electronic strobes

so, you will need to experiment with your electronic strobe for the correct light. My electronic strobe is a strong unit, and if I am closer than twelve feet to my subject, I put a piece of masking tape over the flash area to soften the effect. I don't want to over light the subject.

•I create an electronic strobe system for side lighting, Figure 9-2.

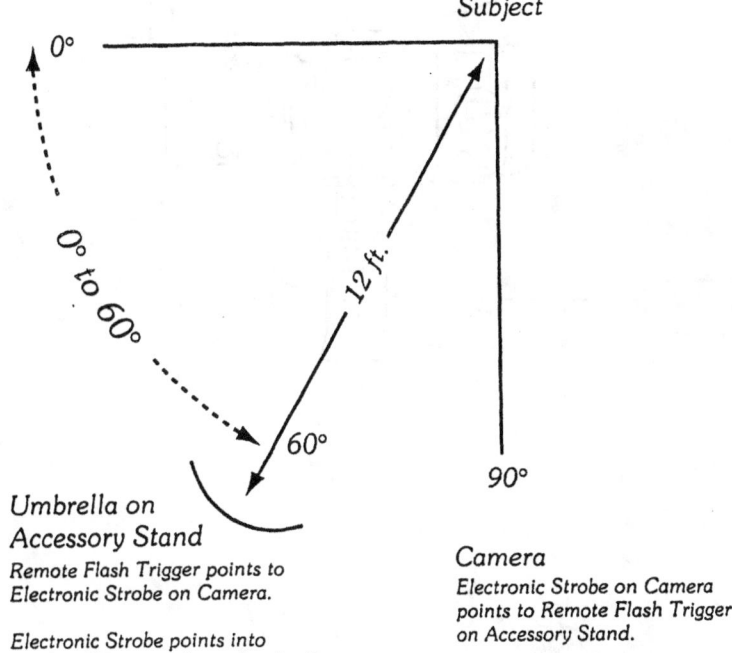

Subject

0°

0° to 60°

12 ft.

60°

90°

Umbrella on Accessory Stand
Remote Flash Trigger points to Electronic Strobe on Camera.

Electronic Strobe points into inside reflective surface of umbrella.

Camera
Electronic Strobe on Camera points to Remote Flash Trigger on Accessory Stand.

Figure 9-2
Electronic Strobe System for
Side Lighting

Your equipment will vary from mine but the system can be applied to your equipment. I assemble my equipment as follows:

•On a tripod I mount the Hasselblad Camera, 150mm lens, warming filter, lens shade with attachment for electronic strobe, connecting cord, and electronic strobe, Figure 9-3.

•On a separate stand I mount an accessory arm, Reflectasol umbrella, Remote Flash Trigger with connecting cord to electronic strobe, Figure 9-4.

Tied to the stand is a twelve foot measuring string. Leg weights can be used to anchor the stand from any unwanted breeze.

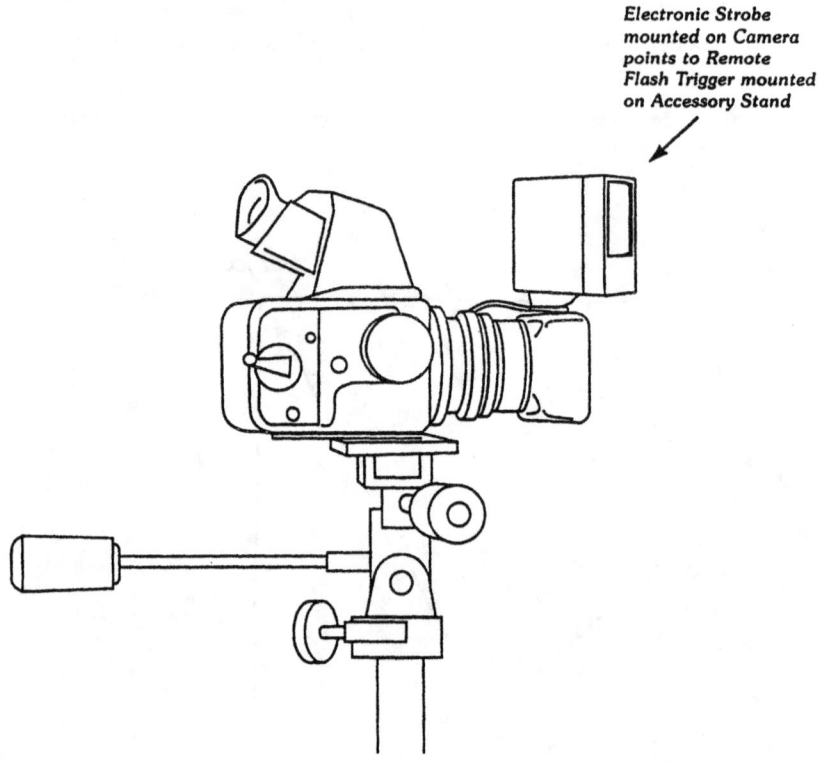

Electronic Strobe mounted on Camera points to Remote Flash Trigger mounted on Accessory Stand

Figure 9-3
Electronic Strobe Mount for
Side Lighting

I place the equipment, Figure 9-2, Figure 9-3, Figure 9-4:

• Set the camera at the preferred distance from the subject who is placed in the desired location for lighting on the face.

• Set the reflective surface of the umbrella mounted on the stand approximately twelve feet from the subject by using the measuring string attached to the stand. The exact footage depends on the power of your electronic strobe. Set the stand at the desired lighting angle ranging from 0 degrees to 60 degrees as demonstrated in Figure 6-4. Raise the level of the umbrella to approximately 2 feet above the subject's head. Adjust the umbrella so the center of the umbrella points to the facial angle to be emphasized, not to the body angle.

• Aim the electronic strobe that is on the camera towards the Remote Flash Trigger on the stand. Be sure the electronic strobe and Remote Flash Trigger are facing each other.

• Fine tune the subject's posing. Check the umbrella stand for precise position by standing behind the subject for the alignment. Focus the camera and make an exposure.

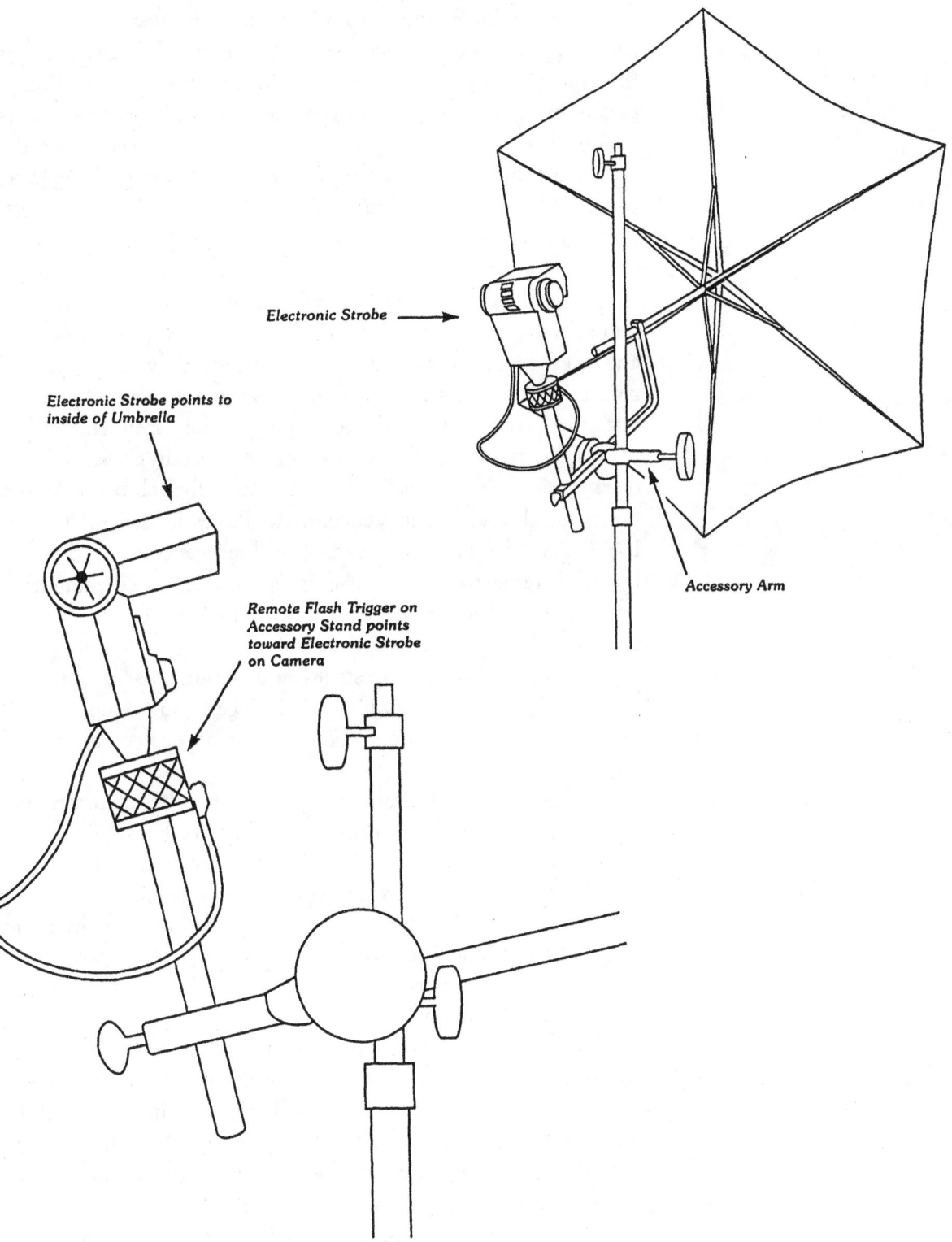

Electronic Strobe

Electronic Strobe points to
inside of Umbrella

Accessory Arm

Remote Flash Trigger on
Accessory Stand points
toward Electronic Strobe
on Camera

Figure 9-4
Remote Flash Trigger Mount for
Side Lighting

• The light from the umbrella is controlled lighting as it falls on the subject. By moving the umbrella stand closer or further from the camera you vary the type of lighting. Be sure the reflective surface of the umbrella points directly at the subject. The flash is weaker at the edges regardless of the reflective surface. Often the preferred lighting is to aim the umbrella so the edge of the lighting pattern falls 4" to 5" in front of the face for a feathering effect. Equipment varies so some experimenting should be done to calculate your exact measurements and positions.

The choices in film are varied. The most important aspect in film selection is its sensitivity to light. Slow films need more light and fast films need less light. I suggest using a slow speed film that gives the best skin tones and still meets your requirements. All film can't meet every requirement so compromise is essential.

Film is constantly being improved. Your choice of film depends on what is available. Years ago when I began classic portraiture I used Kodak Vericolor III, Professional film, Type S, ISO (ASA) 160. The film does not need refrigeration for daily use, but needs refrigeration for long-term storage. Remove the film from refrigeration at least two hours before use to allow time for the film to adjust to the outside temperature.

Presently, Kodak suggests if you used Vericolor III film, you will find Portra 160NC with ISO 160 gives soft, smooth flesh tones. Portra 160NC should be stored at 55 degrees F. but not required.

If there is a significant contrast between the temperature of the room where I store my camera and the outside temperature, to avoid condensation on the lens, I allow my camera to remain outside long enough to reach the outside temperature.

I set the ISO. I load my camera with film after my client arrives at the location because a creative session can be canceled at the last minute. I carry extra rolls of film because film can be defective and I can make errors.

I use the same emulsion number for a consistent dye lot if I am using more than one roll of film in the same creative session.

Before I go on the assignment, I relax and inspire myself by reviewing some of my own work. I say to myself, "Surely, if I made a good portrait once, I can make another good portrait." I have never made the "perfect portrait," but I keep trying.

When I go on an assignment, I try to appear neat, fresh, and stylish. My appearance shows I care and that I am a reflection of the portrait I make. I may not complete the creative session looking neat and fresh because the old adage "Horses sweat, men perspire, and women dew," doesn't hold true. Many times I sweat through layers of my "Flawless Finish" make-up.

When I arrive at the location, I want my knowledge of portraiture, camera, equipment, and seeing adequately defined so using them is second nature.

I want the subject to stay as comfortable as possible. If I am on location at my client's home, I ask him to allow me twenty minutes to set up my equipment before he comes outside. If the location isn't at his home, I arrive at the location twenty minutes earlier than the subject to set up my equipment.

An important step in making a classic outdoor color portrait is where I stand. I look north, south, east, and west, but where I stand becomes the fifth point on my "compass" and the only place that matters. When I move my camera, even an inch, I create another viewpoint. Only when I find the exact position for my camera does the position become obvious to me.

To insure the best depth of field when there is more than one subject, I walk to the side of the subjects, then position the faces as close as possible in a narrow plane, Figure 9-5.

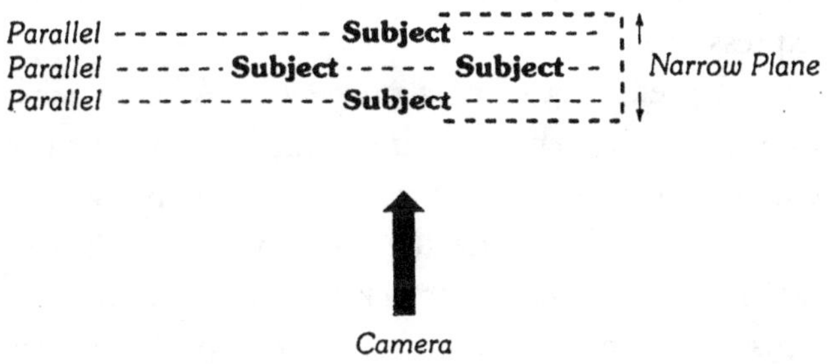

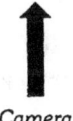

Parallel - - - - - - - - - - Subject - - - - - - - - ↕
Parallel - - - - - Subject - - - - - Subject - - Narrow Plane
Parallel - - - - - - - - - - Subject - - - - - - - ↕

Camera

Figure 9-5
Placing Subjects in a Narrow
Plane

No matter how pleased my subjects feel about posing, the difficult assignment comes in getting them to relax. (I discovered the best way for me to experience the nervousness that a subject feels was to have my portrait made.)

No one poses but the subject. You only suggest positioning. Good posing is learned and/or inherited. Some subjects are more natural in their poses while others struggle. If the subject enters a pose with little instruction, just enjoy the pose. If the subject struggles with the pose, create less tension by not calling attention to the struggle. Instead direct your attention to countless other details. There is a fine line between caring too much for details and overkill.

I don't try to change clients into professional models, but I show my authority. As a way of giving directions, I actually demonstrate the pose. Persons in their own clothes, jewelry, and environment try hard to pose because this is truly a special occasion. Each person has something special, so I take what he offers, such as a good smile and great hair. I apply what I know, then wait for the right expression and moment.

I approach my subject with a pleasant tone of voice and positive comments, such as "This is looking great," "I like what I am seeing," or "I wish you could see this."

I encourage the subject to talk about himself. When I listen, I automatically become a friend. In essence, I match his image of himself with my camera's image.

The type of pose and the number of exposures made depends if you use a book, folder or nothing to show the previews to the client. If the preview book or folder has three sections with two folding wings and a stationery center section, the frame openings in the two wings should have portraits looking to the right and portraits looking to the left so all portraits look into the center. If the book has two sections to open like a book, both sides need to face into the center. If the preview book has many sections consideration is given to the direction each pose is facing and to the equal number of poses such as head and shoulders, partial length, full length, and profile in addition to somber and smiling expressions.

I prefer not using a preview book or folder because I make only one or two poses. I mark the 5" x 5" previews with a black china marker pen to show composing marks. To visualize the composition, I provide the client with two black cropping "Ls" which are two pieces of black framing mat cut into two L shapes. This allows me to show the exact composing marks.

I make only one roll of twelve exposures in a creative session with one person. If I present my client with more than twelve, too many choices are offered. If I make a portrait of a group, I expose as many as two rolls of film because there is more chance for blinking eyes and unfavorable expressions. Often individual portraits result from a group creative session.

I offer a small variety of poses. I divide the twelve or twenty-four exposures into sub-groups based on the number of clothing changes and poses. With one roll of twelve exposures with the subject in two changes of clothing, for example:

• I make six exposures in the first change of clothing. Two are full length, and four are partial poses.

• I make six exposures in the second change of clothing. Two are full length, and four are partial poses.

If I make two-person portraits that are placed together, I want similar backgrounds, image size, and the people facing each other with similar poses.

All of us maintain a "personal territory" or "boundary space" around us in order to feel comfortable. These spaces vary according to the person and circumstances. I must sense the boundary and each person reacts differently to my stepping past this boundary. When I cross the boundary, I lose his spontaneous body movement. If I invade the subject's space, I detect uneasiness by the subject's fidgeting, or an equivalent show of irritation. If the subject defaults, I alone am responsible for getting the subject back in order.

Each person has private and public distances. The closer I move toward the subject, the more intimate the portrait. The further I stand from the subject the more public the portrait.

I begin with the full length pose to allow the subject to be comfortable with me. By the time I set up the partial pose, I am assured the subject will respond favorably.

I can't allow the subject's tension to affect me. I must remain physically and mentally alert. A certain amount of stress is beneficial because it exhilarates. But if the session becomes too stressful my brain functions poorly and I then strive to relieve the stress. To relax, I get my heart pumping by doing a couple of knee bends, take a few deep breaths, swing my arms, and flex my muscles to relax. But, the secret is to engage in this action without alerting my clients. This can be a challenge. Wouldn't you agree?

With experience I have learned to handle the extremely stressful times by anticipating and avoiding the situations. I develop my own defense system. Before the session, I evaluate the most important goals, and if the hundreds of details are overpowering, then I fall back on the main points I am trying to accomplish.

I photograph with few, if any, spectators because when an outsider invades the location, the subject loses spontaneity.

If the subject is a child I prefer the parent not be present. The child's attention is divided because the parent has a different attitude toward the child than me. If the parent pressures the child, I politely ask the parent to leave.

An older child enjoys looking through the camera's viewfinder. After I set up the location I allow the child to look through the viewfinder. Then I begin posing the child.

I take a light meter reading. I set the camera for the shutter speed and aperture setting.

I fine tune the posing by being alert to many details. If the subject is a man in a coat and tie, the shirt collar in the back should be higher than the coat collar. If his coat rides up behind his neck I ask if I can pull the coat down, then have the subject sit on the tail of the coat or I put a clothes pin on the coat and shirt behind the neck to hold them together. A bow tie requires that the shirt in front be tucked in tightly. Be sure the necktie is tight at the collar and straight. I ask the man to unbutton the last one or two buttons of a vest. If not, the vest can look pleated.

I ask the man or woman to empty all clothes pockets to allow the clothing to lay flat against the body.

If the subject is a woman in a full length dress, such as a bridal dress, I increase the skirt volume by shaking the hemline to put air underneath the skirt. I photograph a woman in a full length dress in the full length pose first so the dress won't be wrinkled from sitting.

I check for any dandruff or lint on the shoulders.

I determine if there are stray dogs or cats that can bother us. I take appropriate action. You can imagine what that may be.

If there are any unwanted light spots in the portrait, I use the black head screen mounted on a stand. A photography assistant is useful for holding the screen.

I check the woman's hair style to locate any gaps or open spaces by placing her back to the lighting source.

If there are any stray hairs I ask if I can spray some hair spray on my hand and lightly smooth the hair.

I am constantly aware of changes in the body because the body tends to slump. I don't ask the subject to straighten his shoulders because this only raises the shoulder level. If the body slumps, I ask the subject to put a curve in the arch of his back, because the back bone is the main axis of the body. Then I ask him to imagine he is a puppet held by a string on the top of his head; the string is pulled and all body parts extend upward.

If the veins in the hands appear too prominent, I ask the subject to hold his hands over his head for a few moments. This allows the blood flow to reverse and minimizes the veins in the hands for a short time. If the hands begin to appear stiff I ask the subject to shake his hands to relax them. Then I repose the hands.

A subject's mouth expression can be an open-mouth smile, closed-mouth smile, or serious expression. The open-mouth smile narrows the eyes. Be sure the open-mouth smile does not show any lower teeth. Generally, closed-mouth smiles are best when lips are not too compressed and are relaxed. A closed-mouth smile looks like a smirk if one smile laugh line from the nose to the corner of the mouth is more prominent than the other. The smirk is avoided if the subject's lips are closed in light contact.

Regarding the smile, the old masters determined that the mouth should be at rest in a relaxed manner with only a suggested smile at the corners of the mouth. An open-mouth smile showing lots of teeth tires the viewer eventually. To capture the expression in the eye is more important. Strive for a sparkling eye and relaxed mouth expression. An exception is the subject with a downward curved mouth. A partial smile eliminates the downward curve.

Serious expressions are acceptable. Avoid a stare look by asking the subject to blink with a single closing of the eyes just before making the exposure.

I never ask the subject to smile and say "cheese." Most persons when instructed to smile produce a fake expression. I suggest to the subject that he give me the natural look he wants in the portrait. This usually produces the expression the subject expects.

If the subject's smile freezes, I ask the subject to moisten his lips. This is a good policy because it adds highlights to the lips.

A slight breeze shows movement in the hair. If there is a strong wind blowing the hair there is no real solution except to make the portrait another time.

An easily understood way to achieve the proper tilt of the head is with your hands. Flatten your hands, extend both thumbs from your flat four fingers, touch thumbs together to form a squared U-shape. Show your hands to the subject and gradually tilt your hands in the direction you want the subject's head to move, Figure 9-6.

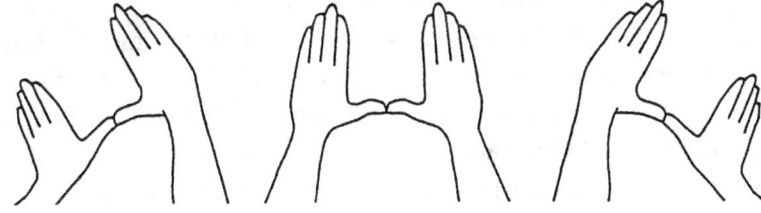

Figure 9-6
To Direct the Tilt of the Head

As an experienced portraitist, I have practiced focusing until I focus with only one turn of the focusing ring. If, for any reason, I focus and refocus, my eye becomes confused. To correct the confusion, I simply move my eye away from the camera, look at something else for a moment, move my eye to the camera, and focus quickly.

I focus on the colored portion of the subject's nearest eye. Dark brown eyes are easier to focus on than light colored eyes.

If I am unable to focus on the eye properly because of too much shade, I simply raise the small, lighter, circled area of the focusing screen to the subject's eye level by raising the tripod, then I focus, and lower the camera to its original height on the tripod.

If I am photographing a group, I focus one-third of the way into the group.

If necessary, the mirror in the Hasselblad camera is released to eliminate any vibration while the exposure is made.

When making exposures I don't look through the viewfinder at the subject but I look directly at the subject to make eye contact. I ask the subject to look at my left hand that is raised slightly above and over the camera. The subject's eyes close slightly when smiling, and this helps open the eyes. My right hand is on the remote control cord.

I capture my subject's expression at his most unself-conscious moment as if I have just greeted him. He then gives me his best look. If I capture him undisturbed, he won't look his best. (Surely, there are enough photographs of mankind at their worst without my adding to the list.)

I make several exposures until I change the pose, or until my subject needs a rest. If a pose feels good to me I don't change, but keep up the rhythm. If the subject freezes, I ask him to move out of the pose and then return to the pose.

At the last exposure, I may say, "This is the last exposure." The subject, knowing the session is almost over, relaxes and usually gives a natural expression.

After the creative session ends which is about an hour, I thank the client, pack up my equipment, and return home.

My creative work continues even after the actual creative session. I send the negatives to the photographic finishing laboratory. When I receive the previews, I evaluate them for the most natural, relaxed, and accurate likeness. I look for the obvious rejects of closed eyes, awkward poses, and those that don't stand up to my peer's criticism. This editing process forces the selection of the best. Later, I look at the previews several more times to discover certain elements I didn't see the first time. I withhold unacceptable previews from the client to simplify the client's selection process.

I then put the negatives in the enlarger and compose appropriately. With a black china marker pen, I mark the previews for the exact composition.

I present to the client the previews with two black "Ls" for illustrating composition guidelines.

When the client and I review the previews I discuss any situations that need enhancing. I use terminology that the subject understands rather than photographic terminology.

Usually the client has discussed with me the location where the finished portrait will be displayed. The guidelines on hanging a portrait are wide because eye sights vary. The smaller the portrait, the closer the viewer needs to be; the larger the portrait, the further away the viewer can be. Additionally, a great amount of detail requires closer viewing while a lesser amount of detail allows more distant viewing.

In helping the client select the portrait size I use the standard for viewing a portrait: the distance between the viewer's eye and the surface of the portrait is two and one-half times the portrait's longer side. For example:

• To view an 11" x 14" portrait, multiply 14, the longest side, by 2.5 to total 35. Your viewer's eye should be 35" from the portrait's surface.

• For 5" x 7," 1 ½ feet
• For 8" x 10," 2 feet
• For 11" x 14," 3 feet
• For 16" x 20," 4 feet
• For 20" x 24," 5 feet

The client will not only consider his own opinion, but the opinions of family and friends in picking the best portrait. I suggest to the client that choosing a preview is easier if he sorts them into groups according to clothes, location, and poses. The more favorable clothes, location, and poses become obvious when compared to previews in each category. A good portrait always shows in the previews and I don't need to offer any explanation.

After the preview is selected by the client, I put the negative in the enlarger and compose the negative on a piece of paper the size of the ordered portrait. I mark the original preview with a black china marker pen to indicate the composition and size. I make notations, with the black china marker pen on the preview, for corrections such as darkening a light spot and airbrushing. These marks serve as instructions for the photographic laboratory printer.

I have never decided about whether to sign my work because my "signature" style exists within the portrait. The portrait, hopefully, stands alone without my signature. In a way, silence offers the best way to enjoy a portrait.

The presentation of the final portrait to the client marks the end of my creative participation.

For retrieval and storage purposes the negatives and previews are filed in archival material. The negatives are housed in archival glassine sleeves. To later identify the selected negative I slightly cut one corner of the negative with scissors at an angle. The glassine sleeves are placed in archival envelopes which are marked with the subject's name, date, location, type of film, and any pertinent information regarding the creative session. These envelopes are filed alphabetically. The previews are filed in corresponding alphabetical order in archival envelopes. Then the negatives and preview envelopes are stored in archival boxes.

My portraits are the documents that tell a story of my era, nation, and culture to future generations.

I make portraits to release creative self-expression and the actual making of the portrait becomes the reward as I see the happiness of the people who view the portrait.

·-T E N -·

JUDGING

Defining Judging

To judge is to offer an opinion on something by giving a response resulting from a first glance or impression and/or by having enough knowledge to give a valid opinion.

After you learn the building blocks to see, create, compose, and add harmonious integrity, how do you know if the portrait is good? To be able to judge the work good or bad is the further unfolding of the world of the portrait.

Judging from a first glance or impression comes from an innate or natural ability. The true judge chooses to refine the personal first glance or impression, to refine the vacillating emotion of admiration and/or repulsion, and to refine the intellect that combines historical knowledge, cultural experiences, and photographic techniques.

Judging a portrait is a personal, subjective experience, not an objective measure. Subjectivity is the result of feelings and thoughts rather than from facts. Most of what one likes or dislikes is subjective. Feelings are either good or uneasy about what is being judged.

Judging a portrait is difficult because the question is "What is best visually?" No saying applies better than, "Beauty is in the eye of the beholder." If the portrait produces any rewards in any form, it's "good." In short, a portrait is good if the viewer's eye and imagination is pleased. When judging a portrait, the first thing to remember is that there is no perfect portrait.

Objectivity results from specific criteria and facts, not ideas or feelings, and should occur without a biased feeling. But to add subjective likes and dislikes, judging, in the final analysis, means simply selecting a favorite.

Any time a portrait is viewed, the viewer automatically becomes a judge with certain standards of taste. Taste is the ability to know what is beautiful and/or proper. Taste is inherited, enhanced by the environment, and further heightened by training the eye to "see." Taste is best when experience, knowledge, and a discriminating eye have been combined and refined. Taste enables the viewer to recognize the good, clear, sophisticated, innovative, and superb, in addition to the bad, morbid, insecure, or garish.

Style is related to taste and results from the viewer's opinions molded by the changing times. The best style of 1900 may not be the best today. Today's best may not be the best in one hundred years. Attitudes in portraiture move in cycles because portraiture style moves in cycles as the popularity of portraiture rises and falls. What is popular one year may be out of vogue the next year. As a judge, the best way to adapt to change is to understand the basic concepts of lighting and posing.

A good portrait satisfies the aware or unaware needs of the viewer such as spiritual, appreciation, beauty, and recording. The good portrait is sophisticated and is simply the image the viewer perceived the person to be in an era, nation, or culture.

A bad portrait doesn't satisfy any needs of the viewer. But what is bad portraiture? Just because the viewer doesn't like a particular style doesn't mean it's bad portraiture. Bad portraiture can include the portraitist not accomplishing his intent, not being worth the effort, and not enhancing the viewer's life.

When a really terrible portrait is encountered, instinctively, the appropriate feeling is to be stunned. It is important to observe bad portraiture because even the worst serves as a bad example. The bad is compared with the good and the best is valued even more. Bad portraiture, fortunately, dies a natural death without having to be condemned.

Portraiture is further evaluated by originality and experimentation. Novelty never stands alone for any length of time because there is no broad base of knowledgeable viewers.

Time is required for a truly fine portraitist to mature and develop a style. We live in an era that often celebrates premature, unearned, and undeserved achievements. Retrospectives are held for thirty year old portraitists whose artistic style has barely begun.

Learning from a Juried Portrait

To have your own work judged in a show enables you to learn from others, makes you competitive with others, and encourages you to "be aware of" more details.

To be judged is a minor part of the artistic process and has little to do with the "filling and emptying" of an artist's soul.

Competition, on the other hand, changes the whole concept of evaluation. You must determine with whom your are competing and how to meet your competition. To enter competitions, you put your portraits before the public, exchange ideas, and have your work evaluated.

When your work is being judged, keep in mind that the judges are given directions and criteria for the judging assignment. These criteria may be artistic merit, originality, technique, and adherence to the classification. The judge in considering if these four areas are good, considers simplicity, contrast, detail, texture, line of design, pattern, depth, movement, spontaneity, and uniqueness.

It takes only a few seconds or minutes for one judge to make an evaluation. But when a group of judges are involved the procedure is more ideal because more time is allowed; judges often have the opportunity to view the portrait several times. This multiple viewing can change the judges' perceptions. The less time allotted, the more narrow the judging becomes.

If you think the judging is to be done hurriedly, you tend to include only excitement and attention-getting devices. But if you suspect judging will include more time, then quality, purpose of creativity, meaning, and originality are included. The elements don't have to be startling, but friendly and appealing.

Also, a judge can unavoidedly include his knowledge of your body of work, which broadly speaking, is all the portraits made by you. However large or varied your body of work, the knowledge of your body of work gives judging a new meaning as the judge can't help but compare the work being judged with your body of work.

Just as there are bad portraits, there are bad judges. Accept the bad judges because they prove that weak criticism dies a natural death.

A good portrait endures even if judged wrongly. If a judge withholds the judging criteria from the viewer, the judge puts the spotlight on himself rather than the portrait. As I said, a good portrait eventually outlives a mistaken judge.

Challenge the judge, for not only is your portrait being evaluated, but the judge is on trial and judging is only as good as the judge.

A judge is not an adversary but will assist in almost every instance. Treat his expertise positively to receive the best from the judge as he determines the best of that show, not the best compared to all he has judged. A judge with broad judging experience doesn't allow his prejudices to interfere.

Judging Your Own Portrait

Judging a portrait, as I've already mentioned, is primarily a subjective experience whether judging your own work or others. However, when judging your own work, you must maintain an objective attitude by separating your emotions from yourself. To accomplish this almost impossible feat, draw not only from judging your own work, but others' work.

To refine the "first glance" judgment of your own work, ask yourself these questions:

• Does the portrait have immediate excitement and allow the viewer to see and feel a little "deeper" than usual? Is the response emotional? Does everyone react differently? When the viewer turns away from the portrait, is the memory of the total portrait?

• Does the portrait elicit a response that lasts beyond the first "blush" of excitement? Does the viewer spend time beyond the first impression deciding why he feels as he does about the portrait? Does the portrait grasp the viewer's attention by creating feelings such as nostalgia, happiness, pity, disgust, or even create curiosity about how the portrait was made?

• Does the portrait not only convey excitement and feeling, but also tell a story that gives the portrait a purpose? The purpose can be multi-dimensional such as beauty, enjoyment, awe, wonder, surprise, spontaneity, and disgust.

• Does the excitement stimulate the viewer to follow the lines of design as they interact?

• Does the portrait attend to the many details you can alter unintentionally or purposely with optics?

• Does the composition remain constant? If the composition guidelines are strictly followed, the artistic merit can be weakened because conformity has become the goal. If the composition guidelines are strongly disregarded, this can detract.

• Does the portrait have good technical quality? Technical quality is not an illusion and should be considered objectively. Poor quality is always noticed and good quality carries the best message.

• Does the portrait possess originality? Does the portrait use the classics as a starting point for originality?

• Does the portrait reveal to the viewer that the portraitist's head and heart work together?

If these above questions are answered in the affirmative, there is an increased chance your portrait is good.

Defining an Excellent Portrait

A good portrait can be good and yet not excellent. Here are a few guidelines on judging a portrait for excellence:

- An excellent portrait isn't always easy to comprehend.
- An excellent portrait isn't always popular.
- An excellent portrait is enjoyed for a long time.
- An excellent portrait is enjoyed by people who are sensitive to style and taste.
- An excellent portrait is enjoyed by people world-wide.
- An excellent portrait uses the classic guideline interpreted by the portraitist.
- An excellent portrait creates a response by stimulating the viewer's sense of sight.
- An excellent portrait isn't confined to one era, nation, or culture for its lasting human qualities.
- An excellent portrait provides a new, valuable experience for the universal viewer.

A FINAL THOUGHT

I am a better portraitist for having written about portraiture.

INDEX

ABOUT THE AUTHOR

NANCY HOPKINS REILY worked for almost twenty years as a classic outdoor color portraitist, making portraits of individuals and families who live primarily in Deep East Texas. She has taught portrait workshops at Angelina College in Lufkin, Texas and has had a one-woman show of her portraits there. Her advance studies include an invitational workshop with Ansel Adams. Reily graduated from Southern Methodist University and lives in Lufkin, Texas. She is also the author of *I AM AT AN AGE* and *JOSEPH IMHOF, ARTIST OF THE PUEBLOS.*

www.ingramcontent.com/pod-product-compliance
Lightning Source LLC
Chambersburg PA
CBHW080900170526
45158CB00009B/2783